AF423034

The Coolest People in the Arts: 250 Anecdotes and Stories

David Bruce

Published by David Bruce, 2022.

While every precaution has been taken in the preparation of this book, the publisher assumes no responsibility for errors or omissions, or for damages resulting from the use of the information contained herein.

THE COOLEST PEOPLE IN THE ARTS: 250 ANECDOTES AND STORIES

First edition. September 18, 2022.

Copyright © 2022 David Bruce.

ISBN: 979-8215993583

Written by David Bruce.

Table of Contents

Dedication

Dedicated to Carl Eugene Bruce and Josephine Saturday Bruce

My father, Carl Eugene Bruce, died on 24 October 2013. He used to work for Ohio Power, and at one time, his job was to shut off the electricity of people who had not paid their bills. He sometimes would find a home with an impoverished mother and some children. Instead of shutting off their electricity, he would tell the mother that she needed to pay her bill or soon her electricity would be shut off. He would write on a form that no one was home when he stopped by because if no one was home he did not have to shut off their electricity.

The best good deed that anyone ever did for my father occurred after a storm that knocked down many power lines. He and other linemen worked long hours and got wet and cold. Their feet were freezing because water got into their boots and soaked their socks. Fortunately, a kind woman gave my father and the other linemen dry socks to wear.

My mother, Josephine Saturday Bruce, died on 14 June 2003. She used to work at a store that sold clothing. One day, an impoverished mother with a baby clothed in rags walked into the store and started shoplifting in an interesting way: The mother took the rags off her baby and dressed the infant in new clothing. My mother knew that this mother could not afford to buy the clothing, but she helped the mother dress her baby and then she watched as the mother walked out of the store without paying.

***

The doing of good deeds is important. As a free person, you can choose to live your life as a good person or as a bad person. To be a good person, do good deeds. To be a bad person, do bad deeds. If you do good deeds, you will become good. If you do bad deeds, you will become bad. To become the person you want to be, act as if you already are that kind of person. Each of us chooses what kind of person we will become. To become a good person, do the things a good person does. To become a bad person, do the things a bad person does. The opportunity to take action to become the kind of person you want to be is yours.

Human beings have free will. According to the Babylonian Niddah 16b, whenever a baby is to be conceived, the Lailah (angel in charge of contraception) takes the drop of semen that will result in the conception and asks God, "Sovereign of the Universe, what is going to be the fate of this drop? Will it develop into a robust or into a weak person? An intelligent or a stupid person? A wealthy or a poor person?" The Lailah asks all these questions, but it does not ask, "Will it develop into a righteous or a wicked person?" The answer to that question lies in the decisions to be freely made by the human being that is the result of the conception.

A Buddhist monk visiting a class wrote this on the chalkboard: "EVERYONE WANTS TO SAVE THE WORLD, BUT NO ONE WANTS TO HELP MOM DO THE DISHES." The students laughed, but the monk then said, "Statistically, it's highly unlikely that any of you will ever have the opportunity to run into a burning orphanage and rescue an infant. But, in the smallest gesture of kindness — a warm smile, holding the door for the person behind you, shoveling the driveway of the elderly person next door — you have committed an act of immeasurable profundity, because to each of us, our life is our universe."

In her book titled *I Have Chosen to Stay and Fight*, comedian Margaret Cho writes, "I believe that we get complimentary snack-size portions of the afterlife, and we all receive them in a different way." For Ms. Cho, many of her snack-size portions of the afterlife come in hip hop music. Other people get different snack-size portions of the afterlife, and we all must be on the lookout for them when they come our way. And perhaps doing good deeds and experiencing good deeds are snack-size portions of the afterlife.

The Zen master Gisan was taking a bath. The water was too hot, so he asked a student to add some cold water to the bath. The student brought a bucket of cold water, added some cold water to the bath, and then threw the rest of the water on a rocky path. Gisan scolded the student: "Everything can be used. Why did you waste the rest of the water by pouring it on the path? There are some plants nearby which could have used the water. What right do you have to waste even a drop of water?" The student became enlightened and changed his name to Tekisui, which means "Drop of Water."

Front Cover Photograph for *The Coolest People in the Arts: 250 Anecdotes and Stories*:

https://pixabay.com/photos/guitarist-guitar-music-instrument-7471606/

***

This is a short, quick, and easy read.

Anecdotes are usually short humorous stories. Sometimes they are thought-provoking or informative, not amusing.

***

Educate Yourself

Read Like A Wolf Eats

Be Excellent to Each Other

Books Then, Books Now, Books Forever

***

Do you know a language other than English? If you do, I give you permission to translate this book, copyright your translation, publish or self-publish it, and keep all the royalties for yourself. (Do give me credit, of course, for the original book.)

Chapter 1: From Art to Conductors Art

Art

• Johnny Brewton is the creator behind the zine *X-Ray*, each issue of which consists of 226 copies, each one at least slightly different. It was definitely an artistic project, and lifetime subscribers included the J. Paul Getty Museum, the rare book department of S.U.N.Y. at Buffalo, and the University of Wisconsin. One contributor was Hunter S. Thompson, who helped create the cover of *X-Ray* #4 by putting on lipstick and kissing a few copies and by shooting a bullet through every copy. (The cover was a photograph of Marilyn Chambers holding a box of Ivory Snow.) Another contributor to *X-Ray* was Charles Bukowski, who impressed Mr. Brewton with his work ethic: Mr. Brewton wrote Mr. Bukowski on a Monday requesting some poems, and by that Saturday — not even a week later — he received an envelope containing some poems. Mr. Brewton says about Mr. Bukowski, "I was amazed at how generous he was — he really *gave back* a lot and supported small presses; he taught me a lot about professionalism and deadlines. He was always on time." Yet another contributor was Timothy Leary. Mr. Leary's publicist, however, in a phone conversation told Mr. Brewton, "Mr. Leary has to charge one dollar per word for articles and stories. Are you sure you want to do this?" Because the zine made basically zero money, Mr. Brewton sarcastically replied, "That fits my budget perfectly! I'll buy one word." The publicist asked, "Which word do you want?" Mr. Brewton replied, "I don't know. Have Mr. Leary decide." The publicist spoke to Mr. Leary, and Mr. Brewton overheard Mr. Leary say, "That's great! Yes! I pick the word 'Chaos' — that's my piece!" Mr. Brewton titled the work "A One Word Dosage from Dr. Timothy Leary" and put a card saying "Chaos" inside a pill envelope — each of the 226 copies of the issue contained the one-word contribution.[1]

• Pablo Picasso was a true artist. Another artist, photographer Yousuf Karsh, once took Picasso's portrait. At first, Karsh was going to take the portrait at Picasso's home, but Picasso's children were boisterous and did such things as ride bicycles throughout the rooms; therefore, Picasso suggested that they meet at his ceramics gallery in Valluris and have the photo shoot there. When Karsh showed up at the gallery with 200 pounds of photography equipment, the gallery owner told him, "He will never be here. He says the same thing to every photographer." Fortunately, Picasso did show up for the photo shoot. Karsh remembers, "He could partially view himself in my large format lens and intuitively moved to complete the composition."[2]

• When Andy Warhola was a senior at Carnegie Institute of Technology (its name now is Carnegie Mellon University), he submitted a self-portrait to the Associated Artists of Pittsburgh Annual Exhibition — the painting was titled *The Broad Gave Me My Face, but I Can Pick My Own Nose*. Perhaps this particular title was a mistake, but Mr. Warhola liked mistakes. The very first time an illustration of his appeared in *Glamour* magazine, his name was misspelled "Warhol." From that time on, he decided to be Andy Warhol instead of Andy Warhola.[3]

• When Renaissance artist Michelangelo Buonarroti was painting his *Last Judgment* on the altar wall of the Sistine Chapel, a man named Biagio da Cesena criticized it because of its nude figures. Michelangelo got his revenge by putting Biagio da Cesena into the painting. In the lowest level of hell, he appears as a horned beast.[4]

• Impressionist painter Claude Monet often painted outside. If you look closely at his 1870 painting titled *The Beach at Trouville*, you can see grains of sand that the wind blew onto the wet paint.[5]

Audiences

• Actress Drew Barrymore comes from two fine, well-loved theatrical families: the Drews and the Barrymores. John Drew's sister, Georgie, married Maurice Barrymore, and they produced three children: Ethel, Lionel, and John Barrymore. All of them became famous actors. In his autobiography, *My Years on the Stage*, John Drew tells of his niece, Ethel Barrymore, appearing in an important role on the stage for the first time. She was nervous, and because she was nervous, she was inaudible. A member of the audience called out to her, "Speak up, Ethel. You're all right. The Drews is all good actors."[6]

• In the 1930s, Ted Shawn and His Men Dancers were subjected to a noisy audience in the Middle West. Mr. Shawn stopped the performance and gave the audience hell, saying, "I have danced before the cowboys of Texas and the hillbillies of North Carolina, and I've never been subjected before to such a rude audience as this." After Mr. Shawn had given the audience hell, the performance continued, and Ted Shawn and His Men Dancers were given an ovation.[7]

• Henry Rowley Bishop wrote the opera *Aladdin* in competition with Carl Maria von Weber's *Oberon*. Unfortunately, his "Hunting Chorus" was very similar to Weber's "Hunter's Chorus." When the audience heard Bishop's "Hunting Chorus" at the premiere of *Aladdin*, they derisively whistled Weber's "Hunter's Chorus."[8]

• Some musicians play from memory as a way to impress the audience, but perhaps the audience ought not to be impressed. One violinist memorized the *Kreutzer*, intending to play it from memory, but he insisted that the pianist use a score so that he could look over the pianist's shoulder at the score if necessary.[9]

• Gustave Mahler sat in the audience at the first performance of Arnold Schoenberg's String Quartet No. 1 in D Minor. The audience disliked it, and Mr. Mahler asked a man near him to stop hissing. The man replied, "There's no need to get excited. I hiss Mahler, too."[10]

• When ballerina and actress Ida Rubinstein performed at the Opera Paris, she would say words of dialogue on stage — words such as "*Où suis-je?*" ("Where am I?") Of course, sometimes someone in the audience would answer, "*À l'Opéra de Paris!*"[11]

Authors

• After Chilean author Isabel Allende's first book, *The House of the Spirits*, was published, her agent, Carmen Balcells, threw a party for her in Madrid, Spain. Many Spanish literary celebrities attended the party, and she was bashful. How to solve the problem? Actually, she didn't solve it — she avoided it. She admitted, "I was so frightened I spent a good part of the evening hiding in the bathroom." As you would expect, she began reading at a very young age. When she finished reading Tolstoy's massive *War and Peace*, her uncle gave her a doll. Her family encouraged her to be creative. For example, her mother allowed her to paint murals on her bedroom walls. (Later, when she was able to drive, she painted flowers on her car. For a while, she had a job translating into Spanish romance novels that had been written in English. However, because she was a feminist, she changed the heroine's dialogue from insipid to intelligent, and she changed the endings so that the heroine became independent and did not need a hero. She got fired. In her own life, she found romance. San Francisco lawyer William Gordon spoke fluent Spanish and met her and asked her to go on a date. After they had had one date, he drove her to the airport, and she asked him if he loved her. She says, "Poor guy, he almost drove off the road. He had to pull over, and he said, 'What are you talking about? We just met.'" She responded by writing a contract and sending it to him. The contract said that they could have a relationship on two conditions: 1) He could date no one but her, and 2) She could redecorate his house. He agreed. By the way, on 17 July 1988, they married.[12]

• Sandra Cisneros, the Chicana author of *The House on Mango Street*, grew up in a family without a lot of money. Her mother made sure that she had a library card, and young Sandra read many books. For a long time, Sandra thought that books were so precious that they had to be kept in a special building — a library. Her love of reading led to a love of writing. She often wrote when she was young, an activity that her mother encouraged. Whenever Sandra, who had two older and four younger brothers, was trying to write but was being bothered by her younger brothers, she would yell, "Mom! The kids are in here!" Her mother would make her younger brothers leave so Sandra could write.[13]

Autographs

• Dancers are asked to autograph strange items. After dancing before President Kubitschek of Brazil and his family, Alicia Markova was asked to autograph one shoe apiece for his two daughters. And in London, a new tomb was needed for a performance of *Giselle*, so décor artist Bernard Dayde stayed up all night constructing one — provided Ms. Markova sign one of her ballet shoes after the performance, which she agreed to do.[14]

• Famous violinist Fritz Kreisler was frequently approached by strangers asking for his autograph. One woman thought that he looked familiar, so she asked someone for his name, then she told him, "I'm one of your greatest admirers; in fact, I ride in one of your cars every day." Hearing this, Mr. Kreisler signed this autograph: "With kind regards, Walter P. Chrysler."[15]

Celebrities

• When she was a young woman, Alexandra Danilova became upset when some men started lying about having affairs with her. Sergei Diaghilev advised her, "Stop crying. What a nuisance. You should cry when they don't talk about you — as long as they are talking about you, you are interesting."[16]

• Some ballerinas are celebrities. In 1978, Natalia Makarova gave birth to her son, Andrew. The guests at his christening included Rudolph Nureyev, Jacqueline Onassis, Anne Getty, and former King Constantine of Greece.[17]

Children

• Many musical geniuses started early in life: 1) Eugene Ormandy loved music from a very early age. When Eugene was age one and a half, his father could play the opening measures of approximately 50 pieces of music, and young Eugene could identify them. Just a few years later, at a concert, a violinist played the wrong note, and young Eugene yelled, "F-sharp, not F-natural!" 2) Even at age three and a half, renowned conductor Herbert von Karajan loved music. Whenever his older brother took a music lesson, young Herbert hid under the piano. After the lesson was over, he came out of his hiding place and attempted to play the notes he had heard while he was hiding. 3) Conductor George Szell's ear was developed at an early age. As a child, he used to listen to his mother play the piano. Whenever she played a wrong note, he slapped her wrist.[18]

• As a 13-year-old girl, Natalia Makarova applied to study at the Vaganova School (aka the Kirov School) of Ballet in Leningrad. She was taken to the Medical Section, which made her wonder because she wasn't sick, and the medical personnel tested her flexibility by twisting and turning her legs in various directions. This so frightened young Natalia that when she was asked for her telephone number, she gave the wrong one. Fortunately, the personnel of the school were able to track her down anyway, and Ms. Makarova received the training that enabled her to become a world-class ballerina.[19]

• David, the young son of pop artist Roy Lichtenstein, once came home from school and said that the teacher had asked the kids what kind of jobs their fathers had. David complained that the other kids' fathers had interesting jobs, but "you're an artist and you can't draw." To show David that he in fact could draw, Mr. Lichtenstein drew Mickey Mouse and Donald Duck. These cartoon characters appeared in his 1961 painting *Look Mickey*, and Mr. Lichtenstein started to become famous.[20]

• Eleanor Peters, who was instrumental in convincing married dancers Marian Ladré and Illaria Obidenna Ladré to start a ballet school in Seattle, Washington, had a lovely apartment on 36th Street in Seattle. The third floor was devoted in part to her son's toy train. (Because there were so many toys in the son's bedroom, there was no room for the train.) Mrs. Ladré noted with amusement that the butler spent more time than the son did playing with the train.[21]

• When lieder singer Lotte Lehmann was a child, she had a very thick pigtail, which she put to good purpose by allowing a small friend to grab hold of it and swing her in circles. By the way, Ms. Lehmann sang in Cuba shortly after the revolution. A notable feature of her bedroom at the Grande Hotel Nazionale was that it had a gaping hole as a result of a shell fired in the revolution.[22]

• As a child dancer, Muriel Stuart impressed Anna Pavlova. While auditioning for the great dancer, Ms. Stuart danced to a waltz. Ms. Pavlova asked the pianist to switch to a polka, and Ms. Stuart immediately changed the tempo of her dancing. Because of this, Ms. Pavlova gave the child dancer the privilege of sitting beside her during the remaining auditions.[23]

• Maria Avelis, who during the mid-1950s was a soprano at the Metropolitan Opera, remembers her start in music. Her sister was taking voice lessons, and she missed a note. Her sister's teacher asked young Maria to try to hit the note, and she did. (Young Maria thought her note sounded like a "howl," but the voice teacher called it "wonderful.")[24]

• Dancer Ted Shawn once gave his wife, the dancer Ruth St. Denis, a peacock as a present. The beauty of the peacock thrilled a neighborhood child — until she heard the peacock's unbeautiful cry. The child turned to Mr. Shawn and, with tears in her eyes, said, "Can't God do nothing perfect?"[25]

Clothing and Costumes

• In her autobiography, *I'm Not Making This Up, You Know*, Anna Russell writes that sometimes during performances she used to wear a gown that had "a big pouffe of tulle at the back of the skirt, making a little train." During an appearance in San Francisco, her accompanist accidentally stepped on the train, pulling out the long length of tulle. Much later, during an appearance in London, Ms. Russell was wearing the same dress, but she had a new accompanist, whom she forgot to warn about her train. Once again, her accompanist accidentally stepped on her train, pulling out the long length of tulle. After the performance, an American sailor came backstage and said that he enjoyed her work, but he especially enjoyed the part at the end, when her accompanist stepped on her train. Ms. Russell explained that that had been an accident, not part of the show, but the sailor replied, "The h*ll it was an accident. I saw you do it in San Francisco."[26]

• Vaslav Nijinsky was dismissed from the Imperial Theaters of Russia in January 1911 because he had worn an "improper" costume in a performance. The costume, which had been designed by Alexandre Benois, did not have trunks over the dancer's tights, although the Imperial Theaters required trunks. In solidarity with her brother, Bronislava Nijinska immediately resigned from the Imperial Theaters, and the two then joined the Ballets Russe. By the way, when Bronislava started her dance studio — Nijinska's Ecole de Mouvement — in Kiev in 1919, the Russian Revolution was in full force. Her students paid for their tuition with such necessities as food and fuel.[27]

\• Judy Garland and Katherine Hepburn appeared in a group portrait of MGM movie stars that appeared in *Life* magazine in 1948. Ms. Hepburn, who was wearing slacks, told Ms. Garland, who was wearing a pale skirt and a black blouse, "I knew I'd be badly dressed, and I knew you'd be badly dressed. The only difference is that you took the time." A later celebrity who sometimes dressed oddly was Bette Midler, who got her start in the gay club known as the Continental Baths, where her many fans frequently wore nothing but towels. For her encores, the Divine Miss M reappeared on stage, wearing only a towel.[28]

• Early in Rudolf Nureyev's career, before he had been accepted into the Leningrad Ballet School, he danced in a sailor's costume in his folk-dance troupe. Because the trousers of his costume weren't ready, he borrowed trousers from another member of the troupe, and as he was dancing, the trousers fell down. By the way, near the end of his career, Mr. Nureyev was often asked the vexing question, "When do you plan to stop dancing?" In answering, he often used the same reply that Margot Fonteyn had used near the end of her career, "I'll stop when the audience no longer wants to see me."[29]

• Copenhagen's Royal Theater has a hole in the floor. The hole, which can be plugged up as necessary, is called a "hand-hole," and it is used to help with a quick costume change on stage. For example, a water nymph may need to be transformed back into an Italian woman before the audience's eyes. Smoke is made to swirl around the water nymph, a hand reaches up from the hand-hole, and the nymph costume is whisked away, revealing the Italian costume underneath.[30]

• Young ballet student Natalia Makarova saw the world-class ballerina Galina Ulanova dance the part of Juliet in *Romeo and Juliet* at the Kirov in the 1950s. Ms. Makarova remembers that at the curtain call Ms. Ulanova wore Juliet's cloak — and in stark contrast to the ethereal quality of Juliet, Ms. Ulanova was also wearing a pair of high-topped winter boots. Because Ms. Ulanova had to catch a train, she had put on her boots in the wings of the theater.[31]

• Rudolph Nureyev wanted to learn dancing at the Kirov. At his audition, the woman ballet teacher Costravitskaya watched him closely, then told him, "Young man, you'll either become a brilliant dancer — or a total failure. And most likely you'll be a failure!" By the way, when Mr. Nureyev danced the part of Albrecht in *Giselle*, he wore a wig that was so blond and curly that he called it his Marilyn Monroe wig.[32]

• Madame Manya was a costumer of genius. She made many costumes for ballerina Alicia Markova, and whenever she decorated a costume with pearls and jewels, she covered the costume with a very fine, almost unnoticeable net, so that no pearls or jewels ever fell to the floor during a Markova performance. Today, Madame Manya's costumes can be seen at the Theatre Museum in London — the inside of each costume is as finely made as the outside.[33]

• Vicky Tiel's granddaughter, Lucie Belle, may have inherited Vicky's love of fashion. When Lucie Belle got a baby brother, she announced that she was going to marry him and therefore needed a red dress that would match her red shoes. Lucie Belle's favorite shoes, of course, are red patent-leather Mary Janes. When the shoe salesman showed her a pair of brown Oxfords, she told him, politely, "I don't think so."[34]

• Ballet dancers go through ballet shoes quickly. In the 1980s, Briar Brownson, the "shoe lady" of the Sadler's Wells Royal Ballet, used to keep on hand 30 pairs of pointe shoes for each woman and six pairs of black and six pairs of white ballet slippers for each man in the company. Whenever her stock of shoes got any lower than that, she grew worried about running out.[35]

• As a young ballerina, Illaria Obidenna Ladré wore the very short tunics that her teacher, Ms. Vaganova, wanted the students to wear. Later, as a dancer for Sergei Pavlovich Diaghilev, her short tunic shocked the wardrobe mistress, who remarked, "Any shorter, and you'd need lipstick!" (At the time, early in the 20th century, lipstick was worn mostly by prostitutes.)[36]

• James Abbott McNeill Whistler dressed eccentrically to attract attention. A fellow painter, Edgar Degas, once told him, "If you were not a genius, you would be the most ridiculous man in Paris."[37]

• Costumes in dance can be shocking. In 1907, Maude Allan danced her *Vision of Salome* in a costume consisting only of strings of pearls that formed a loincloth and bra.[38]

Collecting

• Lynn Peril, publisher of the zine *Mystery Date*, loves books. Her parents read to her frequently when she was very young. Ms. Peril says, "I was never taught to read; I simply woke up one day and discovered I could. I remember going downstairs and telling my mother, 'Hey,

Mom — I can read!'" Her uncle lived surrounded by books. After he died, and when her aunt moved out of the house, her aunt let all the nephews and nieces take the books they wanted. Ms. Peril got a lot of first editions in excellent condition, often with dust jackets, because whenever an author such as Vladimir Nabokov, Flannery O'Connor, or Eugene O'Neill came out with a new book, her uncle would quickly buy a copy and read it. She reads the books, and she enjoys going to an antiquarian bookseller near where she lives, looking at the shelves, and saying, "Hey, I have that book."[39]

• J. Paul Getty once bought a Raphael-like painting for £38 simply because he liked it. Later, the Raphael-like painting was discovered to be a genuine Raphael and not an imitation. Of course, this gratified Mr. Getty — not so much for the excellent investment he had made, but because the purchase had validated his artistic judgment.[40]

• Gertrude Stein and her older brother Leo made many wise acquisitions in art, and soon their house was besieged by visitors who had come to look at their collection. Eventually, to gain some privacy for themselves, they announced that they would show off their collection to visitors only on Saturday evenings.[41]

Competitions

• Adelina Patti and Etelka Gerster were rivals for the prima donna position in Colonel James H. Mapleson's traveling opera company. In Chicago, both singers appeared in Meyerbeer's *Les Huguenots*, with Ms. Patti singing the role of Valentine and Ms. Gerster the role of the Queen. At the end of Act 1, huge bouquets of flowers were brought to Ms. Patti, even though she had had little to do in the first act, with most of the singing being done by Ms. Gerster. Finally, a small basket of posies was presented to Ms. Gerster — and the crowd went wild with excitement and applause. That evening, Ms. Patti swore that she would never again sing with Ms. Gerster.[42]

• Opera/lieder singer Kathleen Ferrier started out as a pianist, but decided to take singing lessons after hearing a singing class and thinking, "I could make nicer noises than those." A friend bet her that she wouldn't have the courage to enter a singing contest, so she entered and won the prestigious award called the Blue Bowl. By the way, Ms. Ferrier once acquired what she called a "half-crown piano." While very young, she had entered a singing contest whose entry fee was half a crown and she had won the prize: a piano.[43]

Composers

• Some music trivia: 1) Many towering geniuses were short. Franz Schubert was 5-foot-2, Igor Stravinsky was 5-foot-3, and Ludwig van Beethoven, Wolfgang Amadeus Mozart, and Arnold Schoenberg were 5-foot-4. 2) John Taylor was a physician who operated on the eyes of the historian Edward Gibbon and the composers George Frideric Handel and Johann Sebastian Bach. In each case, he ruined their eyesight. 3) As a 14-year-old, Richard Wagner wrote a play titled *Leubald* in which 42 characters had died by the fourth act. Many of them reappeared as ghosts in the final act. 4) Ludwig van Beethoven knew that he was a musical genius. To Prince Lichnowsky he once said, "There are and there will be thousands of princes. There is only one Beethoven." 5) You can't always trust signs. George Frideric Handel was born in Halle, Germany. A sign announces that a certain house was his birthplace, but according to composer and music historian David W. Barber, Handel was actually born in the house next door.[44]

• Avant-garde composer John Cage created a piece titled *4'33"* in which the musician sits without playing for four minutes and 33 seconds. This piece was first performed on 29 August 1952, by pianist David Tudor in Woodstock, New York. (The piece can be played by any instrument and by any ensemble.) Mr. Cage also created a piece titled *Imaginary Landscape No. 4* — in it, 12 radios are tuned to 12 different radio stations. The stations are randomly chosen by tossing a coin.[45]

• George Frideric Handel occasionally "borrowed" from other composers. After being told that something he had supposedly composed was actually written by Bononcini, Handel merely remarked, "It was much too good for Bononcini."[46]

Conductors

• Occasionally, conductors have trouble with singers. Once, Arturo Toscanini instructed soprano Geraldine Farrar in how to sing a particular aria, but she ignored his instructions. When he told her again how to sing the aria, she replied, "You forget, Maestro, that I am the star." Maestro Toscanini shot back, "I thank God I know no stars except those in heaven which are perfect." By the way, the premiere of Maeterlinck's *Pelléas et Mélisande* with music by Debussy was given at La Scala — to the hooting of the audience. Throughout the performance, Maestro Toscanini conducted with dignity, ignoring the noise made by the audience, even though it was impossible to hear one note of the music.[47]

• Sir Adrian Boult once accepted an invitation to conduct British music with a famous American orchestra that was known for a few eccentric qualities. Sir Adrian and the orchestra practiced well together, and he was able to remove the eccentric elements of the orchestra's performance and replace them with elements of *nobilmente*. However, at the concert, the orchestra played with all of its original eccentricity and with none of Sir Adrian's *nobilmente*. Following the concert, an annoyed Sir Adrian asked the concertmaster why the orchestra had played one way during rehearsal and a very different way during the concert. The concertmaster replied, "The rehearsal's all yours — but the concert's all ours."[48]

• Anton Horner was first horn of the Philadelphia Orchestra for decades. Because of his great competence on the horn, he was secure enough to stand up to famous conductors. When Leopold Stokowski began to conduct the Philadelphia Orchestra in 1912, he always criticized each performance and told the musicians what they had done wrong. After a few weeks of constant criticism, Mr. Horner spoke up, telling Maestro Stokowski that he should tell the musicians what they had done right as well as what they had done wrong. Shortly afterward, Mr. Horner was moved from first horn to third horn. However, he was so competent a musician that he soon returned to first horn.[49]

• Thomas Beecham once conducted Camille Saint Saëns' Third Symphony in C Minor. Beecham thought that Saint Saëns' tempi had become depressingly slow in his later years, and so he livened things up through accentuation as much as possible during the performance. Later, he asked Saint Saëns what he had thought of the performance. Saint Saëns replied, "You mean, what do I think of your interpretation? My dear young friend, I have lived a long while, and I have known all the *chefs d'orchestre*. There are two kinds; one takes the music too fast, and the other too slow. There is no third!"[50]

• Sir Thomas Beecham was once asked to conduct the orchestra on a ship. Afterward, the ship's captain asked him his opinion of the orchestra. Sir Thomas replied, "Wait until I get ashore first." By the way, Sir Thomas joked sometimes at the expense of great composers. After Sir Thomas had conducted an opera by Mozart, Fritz Reiner congratulated him, saying, "Thank you for a delightful evening with Beecham and Mozart." Sir Thomas replied, "Why drag in Mozart?"[51]

• Conductor Arturo Toscanini once wrote composer Richard Strauss for permission to give the first performance in Italy of Strauss' *Salome*. After receiving permission, Toscanini began to prepare the piece. However, he later discovered that Strauss himself was going to conduct *Salome* in Italy the week before Toscanini was scheduled to conduct it. Immediately, Toscanini took the train to Vienna, where he called on Strauss and said to him, "As a musician I take off my hat to you, but as a man, I put on 10 hats."[52]

• Conductor Arturo Toscanini could be very forceful in his language and behavior toward his singers. At La Scala, a group of singers once complained to General Manager Giulio Gatti-Casazza that Mr. Toscanini was being abusive to them. Mr. Gatti-Casazza replied, "What can I do! He abuses me, too!" By the way, Maestro

Toscanini once said, "I kissed my first woman and smoked my first cigarette on the same day. I have never had time for tobacco since."[53]

• Organist Nadia Boulanger once forced Walter Damrosch to conduct an organ concerto by Aaron Copland by refusing to play anything else. However, Mr. Damrosch got his revenge — after the concerto was finished, he turned to the audience and said, "If a young man at the age of 23 can write like that, in five years he will be ready to commit murder."[54]

• When Antonin Dvorak created his *New World Symphony*, he marked the slow movement *andante*. However, Anton Seidl conducted the movement *largo* at a rehearsal. Hearing that, and liking it, Dvorak changed the tempo to *largo*. Music critic Henry T. Finck writes, "A greater compliment has never been paid to any interpreter."[55]

• Conductor Otto Klemperer disliked being bored. At the end of a boring lecture on composer Paul Hindemith, the lecturer asked if anyone had any questions. Maestro Klemperer stood up, and when everyone looked at him, he asked, "Where is the lavatory?"[56]

Chapter 2: From Creativity to Fans

Creativity

• Artists see and hear possibilities that other people don't see. David Hockney enjoyed driving his car in the Santa Monica Mountains. He also enjoyed listening to music such as Wagner's *Parsifal* while driving. While driving, he noticed that occasionally the music suited the landscape exactly, and therefore he choreographed two drives in which the high points of the music corresponded with the high points of the landscape. He even took some children with him on one of these choreographed drives. They sat quietly during the drive, then told him, "It's like a movie," which Mr. Hockney interprets as "meaning what they saw and what they heard combined into something."[57]

• Window dresser Simon Doonan recommends the use of perishable food in windows despite the presence of mice in upscale fashion shops. For one thing, it makes a window display that people will notice and talk about — forever. For example, "Did I ever tell you about the day I saw a mouse chomping on a piece of cake next to a Prada handbag in a Barneys window?"[58]

Critics

• The Guerilla Girls engage in activism for artists who are women or people of color, frequently by creating posters. The Guerilla Girls wear gorilla masks and are anonymous, taking on the names of deceased famous women creators. As you may expect, they get support from other women. Once, they received this letter from a woman who was a secretary at a museum in New York: "I work for a curator you named on one of your posters. You're right. He's an [*]sshole. Here's $25." In addition, the Guerilla Girls' posters frequently include information about how many women artists are or have been in shows at museums or art galleries, something that requires research. Guerilla Girl "Rosalba Carriera" says that when the Guerilla Girls asked for the bigwigs when telephoning to do research, they often lost time as their questions were evaded. Fortunately, they came up with a way to solve this problem: "Then we learned not to ask for the boss, but just to tell the secretaries and receptionists who we were and what we needed. Like magic, they always gave us the statistics right away." By the way, Guerilla Girl "Frida Kahlo" and other members of the group are working on a way to stop war. "Frida Kahlo" explains, "We want to create the Estrogen Bomb. When it is dropped in an area of violent conflict, men will throw down their guns, hug each other, apologize, say it was 'all their fault' and then start to clean up the mess."[59]

• Carl Sandburg reviewed books and lectures early in his career and movies late in his career. Occasionally, he gave anonymous reviews — sometimes of his own work! Walt Whitman also did this; when his *Leaves of Grass* appeared, he gave it a rave, unsigned review. Mr. Sandburg gave his own lectures and poetry excellent reviews. In October 1907, the editor of a labor newspaper brought Mr. Sandburg to Manitowoc, Wisconsin, to give a lecture. The editor also allowed Mr. Sandburg to review — anonymously — his own lecture on the front page of the newspaper. Mr. Sandburg wrote, "Sandburg proved himself a man of deep thinking ability and great oratorical ability." Mr. Sandburg quoted such reviews in advertisements for his lectures. He also would write blurbs for his own work and use a friend's name as attribution for the blurbs. Mr. Sandburg once said, "I am a ready liar for a good cause." Of course, Mr. Sandburg's lectures and poetry were often excellent.[60]

• In an article for *The Guardian* published in March 2011, critic and writer Germaine Greer explained a few things about art. This is one point she made: "A kid doing graffiti will make no money and could go to jail. There is no truer example of the sacredness of the art enterprise." Another point she made is this: "Most art is bad, but you don't get the good art without the bad. Our best artists make stuff they know is bad; the difference is that they destroy it themselves." As an example, she uses the artist Tracey Emin, who earned an MA at the Royal College of Art. She is a successful artist, and lots of art dealers would love to have the art that she created to get her MA, but they never will. The art did not meet Ms. Emin's high standards, and she destroyed it. According to Ms. Greer, "That's the kind of thing real artists can be expected to do."[61]

• Auditions do not always go well. At the very beginning of her career, modern dance pioneer Isadora Duncan auditioned for a traveling theatrical company by dancing passionately to Felix Mendelssohn's *Songs Without Words*. The manager of the company remained silent for a few moments after the audition, then said to Isadora's mother, "This sort of thing is no good for a theater. It's more for a church. I advise you to take your little girl home." By the way, Ms. Duncan danced from a very young age. When asked when she had started dancing, she always replied, "In my mother's womb."[62]

• In the 17th century, Irishman Michael Kelly composed theater music and sold wine. His wine shop had this sign: "Wine merchant and composer of music." Richard Brinsley Sheridan preferred Mr. Kelly's taste in wine to his taste in music and advised him to change his sign to this: "Merchant of music and composer of wines." By the way, Dr. Samuel Johnson did not especially like music. He once listened to a virtuoso violinist play a pyrotechnical piece. Hearing a companion remark that the violin piece must have been very difficult to perform, Dr. Johnson remarked, "Difficult! I wish to God that it had been impossible!"[63]

• Pianist Vladimir de Pachmann once dined with fellow musicians Leopold Godowsky (an especially good friend), Hans Richter, and Fritz Kreisler. In the course of the evening, Mr. de Pachmann said, "I am happy to be here with my four friends. There are four great musicians in the world. There is me. There is Godowsky. And then there is Bach and Chopin." By the way, critic Philip Hale detested the music of Johannes Brahms. He once proposed that exits in the Boston Symphony Hall be marked, "This Way Out In Case Of Brahms."[64]

• Carl Gaertner, an artist, once attended a recital in which Remenyi, a famous Hungarian violinist, played Bach. Mr. Gaertner hissed during the performance, so Mr. Remenyi asked his critic to identify himself. Mr. Gaertner rose and said, "You play Bach like a fool." Mr. Remenyi remained calm, and merely said, "Perhaps so, but will my critic show me how *not* to play Bach like a fool?" Mr. Gaertner did not rise to the challenge, but simply left — to the laughs of the other members of the audience.[65]

• While Anton Dolin was still unknown, and thus before he became a world-famous ballet dancer, he danced a benefit at the Albert Hall in 1923. An astute critic, Monica Ewer, was in the audience. After heaping praise on his performance, she wrote, "When I am old I hope to say condescendingly: 'The great Dolin? I saw him dance when he was an unknown lad!'"[66]

• Photography pioneer Edward Steichen once took a photograph of famed portrait photographer Yousuf Karsh and his wife outside against a background of magnolia blossoms. Mrs. Karsh complained, "What a pity it is not a beautiful day." Mr. Steichen gently touched her arm, then said, "*Every* day of life *is* a beautiful day."[67]

• Early in her career, soprano Francis Alda sang the part of the Princess in *Marouf* at the Metropolitan Opera. When someone asked why Ms. Alda should be given the part of the Princess, James Huneker replied, "There are two excellent reasons why Alda should sing the role. Her right and left legs."[68]

• A man hired American artist James Abbott McNeill Whistler to paint his portrait, but when the portrait was finished, the man disliked it and called it "a bad work of art." Mr. Whistler replied that he had done the best he could, but unfortunately the man was "a bad work of nature."[69]

• The German painter Adolph Menzel did not appreciate the work of the Impressionists. Looking at a collection of Impressionist paintings (which are now worth many millions of dollars), he turned to their collector and asked, "Have you actually spent money on this stuff?"[70]

• Architect Frank Lloyd Wright knew what he liked — and what he didn't like. The Internationalist movement in architecture led to buildings with exposed gas pipes and exposed heating ducts. Mr. Wright called such ugliness "indecent exposure."[71]

Dance

• Vaslav Nijinsky's *Le Sacred de Printemps* was, in the words of critic Cyril W. Beaumont, "an attempt to show the birth of human emotion in a primitive age." It was very difficult to execute, and when it was unveiled for the first time, it required 120 rehearsals, although only six performances were given. By the way, Mr. Nijinsky used to bow to the audience by simply crossing his arms on his chest and nodding to the audience. According to critic Cyril W. Beaumont, "He never gave the impression that he accepted or demanded applause as his due. He appeared to bow out of politeness to the audience." Also by the way, when Mr. Nijinsky's mental illness first descended on him during a tour in South America, he became paranoid and hired a detective to protect him. One of the detective's jobs was to search each stage for booby traps and for broken glass before Mr. Nijinsky performed.[72]

• The Kirov Ballet of Leningrad once performed a satiric *Creation of the World*. The angels try to tidy up chaos, but the devils keep interfering. God and his cherubim play with the world, which is represented by an inflatable ball. God creates light by using a cigarette lighter to set the sun on fire, and he creates fish by throwing a can of sardines into the ocean. By the way, critics sometimes don't want a black dancer to portray Satan, as Namron did in a 1975 revival of Ninette de Valois' *Job*. However, black dancers also sometimes portray Jesus, as William Louther did in Barry Moreland's *Kontakion*. Also by the way, in 1964, choreographer Kenneth MacMillan had the character God display a Union Jack on his shirt. Why? He explains that God is an Englishman, as everyone knows.[73]

• Anyone who dances the roles of Odette/Odile in *Swan Lake* must be an expert ballerina. In Act 3, the ballerina playing Odile does 32 fouettés — for one fouetté, she makes a complete rotation on her left toe while her right leg kicks in and out at waist height. Cynthia Gregory danced Odette/Odile for 20 years and never missed one of the 32 fouettés she had to dance each time. By the way, at the height of her career as a professional ballerina, Ms. Gregory estimated that she had sewn the ribbons on more than 4,000 pairs of pointe shoes. Also by the way, while dancing solos, the ballerina sets the tempo of the music. In opera and symphonic music, the conductor sets the tempo.[74]

• Peter Martins was a protégé of choreographer George Balanchine. One day, Mr. Martins was making a new work on Suzanne Farrell and a male partner, and he kept saying to the male partner, "I don't want to see you," which meant that he wanted the male partner to contribute to a unified performance and not be a distraction. Ms. Farrell burst out laughing, then explained that Mr. Martins was saying exactly the same thing that Mr. Balanchine used to say. "I know, I know, I can hear him now," Mr. Martins said. "He was so right."[75]

• In *Coppélia*, Franz sleeps for much of the second half of the ballet before waking up and performing some strenuous leaping over furniture while being chased. This sudden action after a long rest can lead to strained muscles, so dancer Erik Bruhn used to cover himself with an electric blanket on stage to keep his muscles warm and ready for action. By the way, ballerinas lead an exhausting life. Karen Kain once fell asleep in front of 3,000 people at the Metropolitan Opera House while lying on the stage in the role of Princess Aurora in *Sleeping Beauty*.[76]

• After ballet dancer Mikhail Baryshnikov defected from the Soviet Union in 1974, he looked around the West for a dance partner, finally settling on Gelsey Kirkland because she was the right size to make a good partner for him. When Ms. Kirkland received a telephone call asking if she would dance with him, she screamed at the top of her voice, "WHAT DO YOU MEAN, *WOULD* I DANCE WITH HIM? OF COURSE I WILL!"[77]

• In the party scene of the *Nutcracker* ballet, the performers on stage appear to be talking together. Sometimes this is not acting — the music by Tchaikovsky is so loud that often the performers feel free to talk. During one series of performances in which ballerina Alice Patelson danced, the production manager had to warn the performers to be quiet during the party scene because their conversations were becoming too loud.[78]

• While Alexandra Danilova was dancing with the Ballet Russe, she was practicing pirouettes with the support of Freddie Franklin when someone startled her. Her arm flew back, hit Mr. Franklin in the mouth, and knocked out one of his teeth. His dentist didn't believe it when Mr. Franklin told him what had happened: "But she's so lovely, so romantic, so ethereal. How could she do such a thing?"[79]

• Dance teacher Nicolas Legat drew well — especially caricatures. Once he learned that Doris Sonne, one of his dance pupils, would be unable to attend his class, so he sent her a caricature of himself crying huge tears into a cup. By the way, Mr. Legat was very strong. His dance studio had a pine floor, and he used to throw pennies so forcefully that they would become embedded in the floor.[80]

• Black ballet dancer Arthur Mitchell danced for the New York City Ballet, then started the Dance Theatre of Harlem. He proved that blacks can dance classical ballet, then stated that he didn't want a dance company of blacks only. He once said, "Now I want a company with two of every race in the world and put them on stage and have them all dancing — a kind of Noah's ark!"[81]

• American ballet master George Balanchine occasionally left talented and gifted dancers on their own. Once, Karin von Aroldingen told him, "You never cared about me." Mr. Balanchine replied, "No, dear — I knew you could do it on your own."[82]

Death

• During World War I, many Americans opposed the playing of German music on patriotic grounds. However, many musicians, including Spanish cellist Pablo Casals, regarded this attitude as nonsense, so Mr. Casals started the Beethoven Association in New York with other musicians who supported the playing of works by Ludwig van Beethoven and other great German composers. By the way, when Mr. Casals was 96 years old, he suffered a second serious heart attack. This made him angry, and he vowed, "D*mn it! I will not die!" However, on 22 October 1973, despite the fierceness of his anger, he did die.[83]

• When Orson Welles died, Joss Whedon, then a university student and later the creator of the TV series *Buffy the Vampire Slayer*, was upset and drunk, and he complained, "This man had so much to say, and society conspired to keep him from saying it for so long." His then-girlfriend, a very intelligent woman, said, "It's interesting that you feel that way about him. I feel that way about the entire history of my entire gender!" By the way, Mr. Whedon wants his tombstone to say, "He was getting better." He says, "Whatever I do, I just want to get better at it."[84]

• Opera singer Mary Garden was in the audience when a crazed man rushed on stage and tried to shoot Jean de Reszke, who was singing the part of Romeo in Gounod's *Roméo and Juliet*. Mr. de Reszke kept on singing as two stagehands grabbed the crazed gunman, disarmed him, and carried him off the stage. Later, Ms. Garden asked him, "Weren't you frightened at all, Jean? He might easily have fired that shot." He replied, "There was nothing I could do but hope that he would not fire. I hadn't a moment's fear."[85]

Education

• When Langston Hughes, the famous African-American author, was in the 7th grade in Lawrence, Kansas, his teacher created a separate row of desks for her African-American students. Langston protested, shouting that she had created a Jim Crow row of desks. The protest was effective: The African-American students were soon seated among the white students. Mr. Hughes attended 8th grade at Central School in Lincoln, Illinois, where he became class poet. For the 8th grade graduation ceremony, which took place on 31 May 1916, he wrote a long poem that was very popular. Why? He explained later, "In the first half of the poem, I said that our school had the finest teachers that there ever were. And in the latter half, I said our class was the greatest class ever graduated." As you would expect, he valued education, and he attended Columbia University for one year. However, once he threw away a number of his books. While sailing to Africa as an employee on the freighter *West Hesseltine* in 1923, he threw away most of the books he had brought on board, saying, "It was like throwing a million bricks out of my heart" and that the books represented "all those things I wanted to throw away." Most of the books were college textbooks from Columbia. One book he did not throw away was a copy of Walt Whitman's *Leaves of Grass*. He wrote, "I had no intention of throwing that one away."[86]

• In 1960, Roy Lichtenstein started teaching at Douglass College (the women's college of Rutgers University). There he became friends with Rutgers art history teacher Allan Kaprow. In a conversation, Roy explained that he was using the paintings of Paul Cézanne to teach his students color. Allan saw a Double Bubble cartoon, and he told Roy, "You can't teach color from Cézanne; you can only teach it from something like this." Allan remembers, "He looked at me with the funniest grin on his face." Roy said, "Come with me." He then showed Allan one of his newest works: an abstract painting in which Donald Duck appeared. Soon Roy began to paint big paintings of cartoons, and soon he began to become famous.[87]

• Dancers very seldom see a dance from the audience's point of view, as when they learn a dance, they watch demonstrations from the rear. According to Peter Martins, "Dancers are always shocked when they see for the first time ballets they have danced in for years from the audience's view." Also according to professional dancers, they always suffer from aches and pains as a result of their profession. Rudolph Nureyev once told Mr. Martins, "If I don't ache and pain, I don't know I'm alive." By the way, Mr. Martins once choreographed a piece that he wanted to title *Giardino di Scarlatti*, but he changed the title to *Sonate di Scarlatti* when George Balanchine suggested that "Giardino" sounded like the name of an Italian restaurant.[88]

• If you want a great education, study under people who really know their stuff. After graduating from art school, Judy Chicago noticed that art galleries featured work that was highly polished and highly crafted. She wanted to learn to do that, and she remembered what sculptor John Chamberlain had often advised her: "What I should do is go to auto-body school. Those are the guys who really know how to paint." Ms. Chicago did exactly that. Her class consisted of herself and 250 men. She says, "I learned not only how to spray-paint, but about respect for the object — that I was actually creating a physical object." For her final examination, she spray-painted a Chevrolet truck.[89]

• Near the end of Ted Shawn's life, Norbert Vesak visited him. Mr. Shawn told him, "Remember, I always said that my heart always beats in 3/4 time? Well, now I even walk in 3/4 time." Mr. Shawn then used the furniture to help support himself as he walked across the room, saying, "You see? Chair, two, three / Table, two, three / Doorway, two, three / Banister, two, three." Years later, Mr. Vesak saw Katherine Hepburn in the play *West Side Waltz: A Play in ¾ Time*. At the end of the play, Ms. Hepburn's character used a walker to get across a room — "clunk, two, three / clunk, two, three" — and she pointed out that now she even walks in waltz time![90]

• Dance teacher Nicolas Legat once saw dance pupil Jack Spurgeon writing down something after class, and he was astonished to learn that Mr. Spurgeon was writing out the complete dance lesson he had just been through. Mr. Legat shook his head and said, "You should never write down classes; just keep creating them." By the way, Mr. Legat made jokes while teaching ballet. Sometimes, a pupil would perform several pirouettes and shower onlookers with drops of sweat. At such times, Mr. Legat would recommend an umbrella.[91]

• Ballerina Patricia Bowman worked with choreographer/dancer Léonide Massine, but he made her angry because he kept talking about Alexandra Danilova and how she did certain steps. When Ms. Bowman finally met Ms. Danilova, she joked and said she hated her, because Mr. Massine had kept talking about how she did certain steps. Ms. Danilova replied that when she worked with Mr. Massine, all he could talk about was how Ms. Bowman had done certain steps — "Patsy did this, and Patsy did that! So, I hate you, too!"[92]

• While in Paris, young Mary Garden looked for a good singing teacher, but they seemed to be in short supply as many of the teachers she considered had freak methods, including one man who asked her to open the front of her dress as she sang — perhaps to study the way she breathed. But one day she and her mentor, Mrs. Duff, visited Professor Trabadello, who told her, "Sing for me in a normal, natural way — as if you were singing by yourself at home." Hearing this, Ms. Garden turned to Mrs. Duff and said, "This is my teacher."[93]

• Lilli Lehmann taught the young Geraldine Farrar. Once, to test her pupil's character, she asked her to show up for a lesson at 6 a.m. Ms. Farrar did show up, with only three hours sleep following her performance the previous night. By the way, Ms. Lehmann and Lillian Nordica once left the Metropolitan Opera at the same time on a rainy day. Ms. Lehmann looked at Ms. Nordica's carriage, then revealed her boots and said, "You ride? I walk," before setting out into the rain.[94]

• When jazz musician Duke Ellington was very young, his mother used to surreptitiously follow him to school to make sure he was safe. Mr. Ellington said in later life, "She didn't think I saw her, but I did." In addition, when school ended, she would be waiting for him at the school door so she could walk him home.[95]

• Although Christian Johannsen was from Sweden, he went to Russia and became an influential teacher of ballet before the Revolution. He did not give much praise, and his highest praise when a student had learned something really well was, "Now you may do that in public" — that is, in performance.[96]

• Vincent van Gogh once accepted three pupils, who paid him in tubes of paint. Unfortunately, his pupils disliked the technique that he taught him, telling him that he didn't paint with the technique that academic painters used. Mr. van Gogh replied, "I scoff at your technique."[97]

• In talking about dance, choreographer Michel Fokine frequently used two Russian words: *naslajdaites* and *laska*. According to impresario Sol Hurok, these words, freely translated, mean "do it as though you enjoyed yourself" and "caressingly."[98]

Fame

• This is a story that the great theater actor Joseph Jefferson used to tell on himself. He had a great success with the play *Rip Van Winkle*, and he was impressed with his own success and thought that every well-informed person knew about his success. After a performance, he went to the Fifth Avenue Hotel, where he was staying, and he got on an elevator with a man who had a grizzled beard. The man asked him, "Are you playing in town now, Mr. Jefferson?" Mr. Jefferson thought that the man must be a simpleton if the man did not know that Mr. Jefferson was currently a huge success in the play *Rip Van Winkle*. They talked briefly, and the man with the grizzled beard got out of the elevator. Mr. Jefferson then asked the elevator boy, "Who was that?"

The elevator boy looked at Mr. Jefferson sadly because of Mr. Jefferson's great ignorance and said, "Why, that is General Ulysses S. Grant."[99]

• In his later life, artist Pablo Picasso was so famous that he needed to take steps to get away from the people wanting to see or meet him. Once, he bought a house near Marseilles, but after remodeling the house and moving into it, he discovered that crowds of people gathered on a nearby hill to watch him through binoculars. Therefore, he never settled there permanently.[100]

Fans

• Science fiction author Ray Bradbury was happy to be famous. He pointed out, "To know you are loved everywhere you go — that's wonderful." One of his daughters, Alexandra, wanted him to use his influence to get her into a sold-out David Bowie concert in Los Angles, and he was willing. He got the telephone number of Mr. Bowie's agent and called him to say that he wanted to buy some tickets. It turned out that Mr. Bowie was a fan of his writing and gave him the tickets and insisted on meeting him after the concert. So there Mr. Bradbury was, backstage, talking with Mr. Bowie and being swarmed by other fans of his writing: John Belushi, Ringo Starr, Bette Midler, and Neil Sedaka. Mr. Bradbury says, "My daughter was standing there, like, 'You know, this is just my father.'" Another encounter, among many more, occurred when he was standing on a corner in Beverly Hills and Sidney Poitier drove by and yelled at him, "Mr. Bradbury, I'm Sidney Poitier and I love you." One final story: During the time he was writing *Fahrenheit 451*, he was waiting for a bus at a stop. A young man came to the bus stop. He was carrying lots of books — science books. Mr. Bradbury asked him if he belonged to the UCLA science fiction club. The young man replied that he did, and Mr. Bradbury asked who were his favorite authors. They were Asimov, Clarke, Bradbury ..." and Mr. Bradbury asked, "Oh! Do you like Bradbury?" The young man did: "Very much." Mr. Bradbury asked, "Would you like to meet him?" Of course, the young man did, and Mr. Bradbury introduced himself. They continued talking, and it turned out that the young man lived in Pica de Via, Havana, Cuba, and that his last name was Hemingway. The young man was Ernest Hemingway's son![101]

• When future comic artist Phoebe Gloeckner was 16 years old, she sent a fan letter to comic artist Aline Kaminski Crumb to say, "Dear Aline, I love your work." Aline was kind enough to write back. Later, Aline's boyfriend and future husband, the famous comic artist R. Crumb, played with a band called the Cheap Suit Serenaders in a club in San Francisco, Phoebe's home city, and Phoebe's mother took Phoebe to the concert. During a break, Phoebe's mother spoke to R. Crumb: "My daughter sent your girlfriend a fan letter. She really likes you guys." Amazingly, R. Crumb replied, "Is her name Phoebe? That was the only fan letter Aline ever got from a girl."[102]

• After dancing the first act of *Giselle* in Mexico, Alicia Markova was surrounded by eager souvenir-seekers who had danced the roles of the peasants in Act 1 and who began to snip off locks of her hair. Her sister, Doris, pleaded with them to leave some hair for the second act, but Ms. Markova was able to stop them only by promising them souvenirs from her dressing room. After the ballet, the souvenir-seekers descended on her dressing room and carried away hairnets and powder puffs and other small items.[103]

Chapter 3: From Fathers to Mishaps

Fathers

• When Latina author Sandra Cisneros speaks to young children, sometimes she will show them her 5th-grade report card, which lacks A's. She says, "I have C's and D's in everything .... The only B I had was in conduct. But I don't remember being that stupid." (Later, some teachers encouraged her.) Stupid she is not. In 1995, she won a MacArthur Foundation grant, aka a Genius Grant. She did go to college, something that her father did not oppose — chiefly because he regarded college as a good place for a woman to find a husband. Getting her father's approval of her writing is one of her greatest accomplishments in life. One Christmas, two years after her father had a stroke, she visited him and gave him one of her stories — translated into Spanish — to read. He laughed in all the right places, and he asked if some of the characters were based on people he knew. She remembers, "When he was finally finished [reading the story], after what seemed like hours, my father looked up and asked, 'Where can we get more copies of this for the relatives?'"[104]

• When Alicia Markova, nee Alicia Marks, was eight years old, she danced briefly for Anna Pavlova at the great Russian ballerina's apartment. Young Alicia noticed that Ms. Pavlova was wearing mauve clothing, and mauve instantly became her favorite color. After Alicia had danced for Ms. Pavlova and had received some valuable advice, the great Pavlova rubbed her down with eau de cologne and lectured her about the importance of a dancer's avoiding colds. As Alicia and her father were going home after meeting Ms. Pavlova, they stopped at a drugstore, where her father bought her a bottle of eau de cologne with a mauve bow.[105]

• When World War II broke out, a call went out to the Navajo Nation for volunteers to join the war effort for an important assignment. Carl Gorman, the father of Navajo artist R.C. Gorman, volunteered, enlisting in the United States Marines. Carl was actually too old to enlist, being one year older than the age limit of 35, but he simply altered his birth certificate and enlisted anyway. He became one of the famed Navajo Code Talkers who created a code that the Japanese were unable to break. Later, he became an artist, exhibiting in several two-man shows with his son.[106]

• Isaac Asimov's father was proud of him and would not let him read such pulp magazines as *Weird Tales* and *Thrilling Stories* because in his opinion they were trash. However, he did let Isaac read *Science Wonder Stories* because it had "Science" in the title. This soon became some of Isaac's favorite reading. As a child, Isaac was sometimes unusual. He liked cemeteries because they were peaceful and quiet. However, a caretaker once asked him to stop whistling when he was in the cemetery because he was upsetting mourners.[107]

Flowers

• After witnessing a particularly good performance, balletomanes often throw flowers — which sometimes leads to problems. A balletomane once threw a "remarkably solid and heavy water lily" which hit Margot Fonteyn in the chest. Another regular ballet-goer discovered that flowers were easier to throw when they were weighted, so Ms. Fonteyn quickly learned to keep an eye in his direction whenever she came out for bows after a performance.[108]

• A reporter once interviewed ballerina Anna Pavlova at her home, Ivy House, in England, where he was surprised by the scent of mimosa, because the mimosa tree was not in flower then. The mystery was cleared up where they entered the conservatory, in which stood a flowering mimosa tree.[109]

Food

• Andy Warhol worried about gaining weight. He liked expensive Teuscher chocolate, but he never swallowed it. Instead, he would enjoy chewing it up, and then he would spit it into a napkin. Mr. Warhol also had his own way of eating in expensive restaurants. He said, "When I order in a restaurant, I order everything I don't like, so I have a lot to play around with while everyone else eats. Then, no matter how chic the restaurant is, I insist that the waiter wrap the entire plate up like a to-go order." Mr. Warhol then left the food in a place where a homeless person would find it and eat it. While Mr. Warhol was still alive, quite a few homeless people in New York found a Grenouille dinner on a window ledge.[110]

• Douglas Fairbanks, Jr. and his wife once dined with Fred Astaire, who kept his head bent over his bowl of soup. They asked if something was wrong, and Mr. Astaire replied, "Can't you notice anything?" They said that they could not, and he said, "I've got a new toupee and I wondered if it showed." By the way, according to clothes designer Bob Mackie, Mr. Astaire always wore long underwear while performing his dance numbers in his many movies — the long underwear absorbed his sweat. Also by the way, Mr. Astaire was not a reader. He once asked his son-in-law about the story of *Romeo and Juliet*. His son-in-law explained that it was like *West Side Story*.[111]

• At a hotel in Buffalo, New York, a couple of members of the Merce Cunningham dance troupe had a large can of sardines for breakfast on the eighth floor. They ate all but five of the sardines, which they then flushed down the toilet. On the first floor, dancer Sandra Neels went to the ladies room. Floating in a toilet bowl were two of the sardines.[112]

• When David Niven, Jr. opened a restaurant in London — Drone's — he decorated it by putting baby pictures of famous movie stars on its walls.[113]

Gays and Lesbians

• Do writers have rivalries? According to gay author Edmund White, the answer is yes. Long ago, gay author Gore Vidal dined with publisher Jonathan Burnham at the River Café. On the table were tall bottles of wine as well as tall bottles of olive oil. Mr. Vidal mistook a bottle of olive oil for a bottle of wine, poured olive oil in his glass, and took a drink. He sputtered and then said to Mr. Burnham, "You saw that and you didn't stop me. You want me to die so your writer Edmund White will be King Fag!"[114]

• Rudolf Nureyev once went to a see a controversial play about homosexuality that was running in London's West End. During intermission, he went to the restroom. A reporter saw him, and sensing a story, asked him, "Aren't you Rudolf Nureyev?" Mr. Nureyev replied, "Not at the moment," then vanished.[115]

Gifts

• Ronald Searle created cartoons for *Punch* and other media. As a boy, Gerald Scarfe, who also became a cartoonist, idolized him. Young Gerald found out where Mr. Searle lived, and he rode his bike there to visit him. Unfortunately, he was too shy to actually ring the bell and so he did not then meet the great man. Fortunately, as a married man, Mr. Scarfe was able to meet him. Mr. Scarfe explains, "A few years later, my wife, Jane Asher, organized a secret meal for my birthday at this exclusive restaurant in Provence. When we walked in, the only other people there were Ronald and his wife. It turned out they had lived in this town for years. A beautiful little package sat on the table, all done up with ribbon. I said, 'Oh, is this for me?' And Ronald said, 'Yeah, it's nothing.' So I opened it, and there was a brass doorbell with a note saying, 'Please ring any time.'"[116]

• In 1939, soprano Marjorie Lawrence made a triumphant return to her native Australia. In an interview, she mentioned that while living abroad, she had missed eating a particular Australian dish — rabbit pie. In Melbourne, she was given an enormous rabbit pie that was so artistically wrapped up in cellophane and red ribbon that she was shocked when she opened it up and discovered what it was.[117]

Good Deeds

• During the winter of 1882-1883, conductor Anton Seidl was asked to give a concert in Berlin, Germany, to raise money for the victims of a flood. He did, and some ladies of the aristocracy gave him a very expensive watch decorated with diamonds. The Empress Augusta Victoria also gave him a dedication in her own handwriting. Mr. Seidl said that the dedication was thanks enough to him and would be a family heirloom, but he requested that the watch be sold and the proceeds be added to the funds raised to relieve the victims of the flood. Mr. Seidl did other good deeds as well. He sometimes declined to be paid for his work if he felt that a certain concert had not raised enough money for the managers behind it. At charity concerts, he would conduct for free, but he insisted that the musicians whom he conducted must be paid. According to his wife, Auguste, Mr. Seidl gave away much money and clothing to those in need. For example, a person might tell him that he could get a certain job if he had better clothing, and Mr. Seidl would give that man some of his own clothing. His wife wrote about his clothing, "I was sometimes compelled, when all the half-used clothes had been disposed of, to give away even the new ones."[118]

• Conductor Artur Rodzinski got along very well with the musicians of the New York Philharmonic. When his wife returned from the hospital with their second child, several musicians played Wagner's *Seigfred Idyll*, which the composer had written for his own wife and their new son, Seigfred.[119]

Husbands and Wives

• After George Orwell's first wife, Eileen, died, he kept her jewels and her jewelry box. Sally, the eight-year-old daughter of Susan Watson, the housekeeper he had hired, asked him what he was going to do with the jewels. Mr. Orwell replied, "I'm saving them for a rainy day." Sally then asked what he would do with them on a rainy day. He thought a moment and said, "Why, I think I'll give them to you, Sally." And he did. By the way, Eileen had standards in her home life. During World War II, Mr. Orwell's bad lungs and a previous injury kept him out of the army, but he did join the Home Guard to protect England. To educate himself, he studied explosives and weapons. Eileen told him, "I can put up with bombs on the mantelpiece, but I will not have a machine gun under the bed."[120]

• Often, people said to Enrico Caruso's wife, Dorothy, "It must be wonderful to be married to the greatest singer in the world." She always replied, "Yes, it is." In her biography of her husband, she added, "And it was, but only because he happened to be Enrico. He was the greatest person in the world — and he sang, too." By the way, Mr. Caruso's vocal cavities were extraordinary. His wife reports that he could put an egg in his mouth, then close his lips, and no one would know the egg was in there.[121]

• Dancer Isadora Duncan once propositioned playwright George Bernard Shaw, saying that they should have a child together because he had a wonderful brain and she had a wonderful body. Mr. Shaw turned her down, saying, "Suppose it has my body and your brain?" She also propositioned Maurice Maeterlinck, who also turned her down, saying, "I am honored, Madame, but you must consult my wife."[122]

Illnesses and Injuries

• Early in his career Rudolf Bing auditioned many opera singers as part of his job, and all of the opera singers thereafter felt entitled to stop by his office and ask if there was any work for them. This led to a problem because Europeans have a custom of shaking hands when they enter or leave a room, and in the summer Mr. Bing was shaking hundreds of sweaty hands a day. To combat this problem, he put up a sign on the door of his office: "During the summer months, it would be appreciated if you refrained from handshaking." However, the union he worked with regarded his attitude as undemocratic, and the sign came down.[123]

• Colonel James H. Mapleson once received word that mezzo-soprano Sofia Scalchi was ill and unable to sing in an opera scheduled that night. He and a physician therefore went to Ms. Scalchi's hotel apartment to ask what they could do for her, but just before they arrived at her door, a dinner of roast duck and lobsters was delivered to her apartment. Colonel Mapleson waited for the dinner to get started and after hearing the sound of laughter, he and the physician entered her apartment. No longer able to claim that she was ill, Ms. Scalchi sang that night.[124]

• In Havana, Pasquale Brignoli was disappointed with the audience's applause one night and therefore decided that he would claim that he was ill and so could not sing the following night. A physician examined him, saw that he was not ill, and to teach him a lesson, looked very serious and told him that he had yellow fever. Frightened, Mr. Brignoli immediately said that he was not ill, and he went on stage and put on an electrifying performance that resulted in the kind of applause that he most desired.[125]

• In 1992, Barneys window dresser Simon Doonan created a controversy when he used Magic Johnson as the subject of one of his celebrity windows. Magic had recently been diagnosed with HIV, and so the window focused on safe sex. People objected because a small Christmas tree used in the display was decorated with miniature basketballs and gold-wrapped condoms. Mr. Doonan defended the exhibit by saying that he and Magic were trying to save lives.[126]

• Margot Fonteyn once was surprised to find out that a man she had thought was half-Oriental was actually 100% Panamanian. It turned out that as a boy he had lived in Japan. His face was injured in an earthquake, and the Japanese doctors performing plastic surgery on him had given him an Oriental appearance.[127]

• In 1953, the National Institute of Fine Arts gave Mexican artist Frida Kahlo a one-person show — a great honor. She was ill at the time of the exhibit, but she attended anyway, arriving in an ambulance. Once inside the building where the exhibit was located, she lay on a bed.[128]

• Dancers often are able to dance with injuries through a kind of mind-over-matter discipline. Oleg Tupine once had a broken kneecap as he danced the Prince in *Swan Lake*. During the performance, he felt no pain; after the performance, he couldn't walk.[129]

Insults

• Sophie Arnould was noted for her ability to give witty insults, but occasionally she was the recipient of a witty insult. For example, when the Abbé Galiani was asked what he thought of Ms. Arnould's singing, he replied, "It is the finest asthma I ever heard." By the way, Ms. Arnould once met Voltaire, who told her, "I am 84 years old, and I have committed 84 follies." She replied, "A mere trifle. I am not yet 40, and I have committed more than a thousand."[130]

• S.N. Behrman tells this anecdote about Oscar Levant: He was talking to Mr. Levant about a mutual acquaintance, and Mr. Levant said that he had walked with him recently and found him to be a good companion. This surprised Mr. Behrman, as Mr. Levant had previously said insulting things about this acquaintance. Mr. Levant replied, "Well, you know I hate 'em 'til they say hello to me."[131]

Jokes

• The wonderful comedian Jonathan Winters sometimes jokes about fishing with dynamite. Believe it or not, this happens in real life. Choreographer Léonide Massine bought some islands in Italy, and for a few weeks he was surprised to hear explosions near his islands. Eventually, he closely observed a fishing boat. One of the two men on the boat threw something overboard, there was an explosion, and the fishermen began gathering the dead fish. That was how Mr. Massine learned that they were fishing with dynamite.[132]

• When lieder singer Lotte Lehmann was performing at the Hamburg Municipal Theater early in her career, she worked with two practical jokers: Max Lohfing and Bobby vom Scheidt. In the second act of *Heimchen am Herd* (*The Cricket on the Hearth*), they tied her to her seat with knitting yarn, then waited for the moment when she was required to stand up on stage.[133]

• Sir Malcolm Sargent once made a concert tour in Israel during a time of hostility. While visiting the Gaza Strip, his jeep was shot at by the Arabs. Safely back home, he told his friend and fellow conductor Sir Thomas Beecham about the incident. Sir Thomas joked, "I had no idea the Arabs took music so seriously."[134]

Language

• Many musicians use language well: 1) Sir Malcolm Sargent was once asked what a musician needed to know to play the cymbals. He replied, "Nothing — just when." 2) Sir Thomas Beecham was once asked what he would do after the opera season ended. He replied, "I propose to go shooting — shooting anyone who mentions music." Sir Thomas also once scolded the choir at a rehearsal of Handel's *Messiah*: "When you sing, 'All we like sheep have gone astray,' might we, please, have a little more regret and a little less satisfaction?'" 3) Arturo Toscanini was not shy in criticizing his orchestra when he felt the musicians deserved it. He once shouted at the members of his orchestra, "Assassins!"[135]

• The Nicholas Brothers, an African-American dance act, performed in a show called "Babes in Arms" where they sang a song titled "All Dark People Is Light on Their Feet," but their mother told them on opening night not to sing it that way, but instead to sing "All Dark People *Are* Light on Their Feet." Afterward, the stage manager told them that they were singing it wrong and they should sing "is" and not "are," but Fayard Nicholas said about the Nicholas Brothers' version, "That's the way I talk."[136]

• Marius Petipa choreographed *Swan Lake*. A Frenchman, he went to Russia, where he lived for decades but never mastered the language. To dancers who made mistakes in rehearsal, he said something in Russian, which, translated, was this: "Stop, stop, what miserable madam, what you are bad cucumber."[137]

• Sometimes, not knowing a language well may be an advantage. Arturo Toscanini was displeased with the performance of a musician so he ordered him out of rehearsal. At the exit, the musician turned around and shouted, "Nuts to you!" Mr. Toscanini remained firm and said, "It is too late to apologize."[138]

Media

• Famed conductor Arturo Toscanini disliked giving interviews and to get out of giving them, he occasionally played tricks on reporters. Samuel Chotzinoff, the music critic of the *New York World*, once had an interview with Mr. Toscanini, but he was surprised that the Maestro had only a very weak grasp of English. There was nothing to do but to give up on the interview and leave, which Mr. Chotzinoff did. Later, Mr. Chotzinoff found out that Mr. Toscanini spoke English much better than he had pretended. Eventually, the two men became friends, and Mr. Toscanini was pleased with Mr. Chotzinoff's praise of his acting ability as demonstrated the first time they met.[139]

• In January 1933, the great dancer Bill Robinson, aka Mr. Bojangles, was dancing at the Loews State Theater in New York, when a rat made its way onstage. At first Mr. Bojangles ignored the rat, but members of the audience began to see it and started screaming. Mr. Bojangles knew that the audience would panic, so he picked up a block of wood and began dancing toward the rat. In the middle of the stage, he threw the block of wood at the rat, wounding it, then ran over to it and brained it with the wood — to the orchestra's long drumroll followed by clashing cymbals. The newspapers the next day gave much play to the story.[140]

• Grandma Moses grew up in and loved the country. She once stopped in New York City on her way to accept an achievement award from the Women's National Press Club in Washington, D.C. Reporters interviewed her, and she told them, "It's nice to be here, but the city doesn't appeal to me." They asked, "As picture material?" She replied, "As any material."[141]

• American dance pioneer Ted Shawn once danced a duet with Martha Graham. The dance was Spanish, and his pants split with a loud noise. The next day, a reviewer wrote that the splitting of the "incredibly tight Spanish trousers" was something he had prayed all his life to witness.[142]

Mishaps

• Despite his obvious high intelligence, Isaac Asimov could be absent-minded. When he was married to his first wife, he once took a bill to the gas company and complained about how much it was. He said, "We have never used enough gas to bring us up to the minimum. We have no children. We both work. We cook perhaps four meals a week. How can we possibly get a gas bill for $6.50? I *demand* an explanation." The gas-company employee had a good explanation: "This is an *electric* bill." By the way, television reporter Walter Cronkite once interviewed Mr. Asimov, who wanted to tell him, "My father will be very thrilled, Mr. Cronkite, when he finds out you've interviewed me." However, he was afraid of sounding immature and so refrained from saying it. During a break in the filming, Mr. Cronkite said to Mr. Asimov, "Dr. Asimov, my father will be very thrilled when he finds out I've interviewed you."[143]

• While performing Brünnhilde in Wagner's *Götterdämmerung* in the Vichy Opera House, Australian soprano Marjorie Lawrence was determined to be on a live horse — something she had previously done to great effect at the Metropolitan Opera. However, the Vichy Opera House did not have its own stable, so an army horse with close-cropped tail and mane would have to play Grane. Because Grane must have a long, flowing tail and mane, an artificial tail and mane was used. At the performance, all seemed to be well. Grane swished its long, flowing tail around, and the scene seemed to be set for a magnificent departure from the stage. However, Ms. Lawrence heard laughter as she rode off — Grane had lost its artificial tail.[144]

• When Peter Martins first began performing with the New York City Ballet, he had to learn several ballets very quickly. Often, he learned a ballet during a day, then had to perform it later that night.

On one occasion, he was dancing with Suzanne Farrell. He had five entrances and exits. The first four entrances went well, but he forgot about the fifth. For support, Ms. Farrell stretched out her hand, which Mr. Martins was supposed to take, but Mr. Martins was offstage, so Ms. Farrell fell on her face. To the audience, it looked as if Ms. Farrell had committed the fault. According to Mr. Martins, "She was furious with me about that for a whole week."[145]

• A mishap occurred when Rudolf Nureyev toured with the Australian Ballet. Usually, when a mishap occurs, it is ignored, but Mr. Nureyev often chose not to ignore his own mishaps. The wooden floor was slippery, and during a solo, Mr. Nureyev ended up flat on his back. He got up, went off the stage, then returned and performed the solo perfectly, starting at the beginning. The audience cheered his commitment to perfection. By the way, after Mr. Nureyev had spent his first day as director of the Paris Opéra, Erik Bruhn called him to ask how the day had gone. Mr. Nureyev replied, "Just fine — I only got angry three times."[146]

• In Amsterdam, Anne-Marie Holmes danced the title role of *Giselle*. However, the National Ballet of Holland used a different grave than the one she was used to. The cover to its grave opened in the middle instead of to the side. Ms. Holmes wanted to be sure that her skirt would not get caught in the grave cover so she leaned forward; she was successful in that the grave cover did not close on her skirt — instead, it closed on her nose. Fortunately, the stagehands heard her moan, so they lifted the cover enough for her to get her nose free. Otherwise, the otherworldly spirit that was Giselle would have had an embarrassing time in front of the audience.[147]

• Anna Pavlova expected a lot from her students, even the very young ones. Occasionally, she would become impatient and the students would begin crying. At such times, Ms. Pavlova's husband, Victor Dandré, would calm the students by giving them peaches and taking them into the garden to look at Ms. Pavlova's pet swans. By the way, even at age 14, Anna had presence of mind while on stage. At her first public performance, she pirouetted with such energy that she lost her balance and fell. She stood up again, curtsied to the audience, then continued her dance.[148]

• Alicia Alonso and Igor Youskevitch were a great ballet dance team during the 1950s, but even they occasionally ran into problems. While dancing together in the *Black Swan* pas de deux, Mr. Youskevitch became overly athletic in his lifts of Ms. Alonso, so she complained to him in an aside at the end of their dance that he had handled her as if she were a sack of potatoes. This image was so different from that of the swan she was supposed to be that they startled giggling and were just saved from ruining the drama of the dance by the fall of the curtain.[149]

• In decades of performing, perhaps the worst stage that Alicia Markova ever performed on was in Mozambique in 1945. The floor of the stage was so rotten that a leg of a piano placed on center stage for a solo went right through a board. During their performance, Ms. Markova and her dance partner avoided the hole as best they could. Afterward, they discovered that the last time the stage had been used was when Anna Pavlova danced on it — in 1924.[150]

• Irina Baronova was one of the three Russian "baby" (that is, teenage) ballerinas of the 1930s. Once she was dancing for the King and Queen of England. Being eager to make a good impression, she threw all her energy into a jump, turned upside down, fell on her head — and was knocked unconscious. Another baby ballerina, Tatiana Riabouchinska, finished the dance for her.[151]

• Theodore Thomas was a conductor who did much to introduce Americans to good music. He enjoyed telling an anecdote about a near-sighted trombonist who made a terrible error during rehearsal. Mr. Thomas asked what had happened. The trombonist explained, "Excuse me! I didn't have on my spectacles. A fly sat down among my notes, and I played him."[152]

• When Anna Pavlova and her company danced *Don Quixote*, a real horse played Rocinante. Although the horse was well taken care of, when it was made up for its role it resembled the broken-down nag Cervantes had written about. In fact, in Great Britain, members of the audience complained to the Royal Society for the Prevention of Cruelty to Animals.[153]

• In Blackpool, England, during the days of the heavy bombing of London in World War II, the London Philharmonic Orchestra played Tchaikovsky's *1812 Overture*. Unfortunately, when they used the sound effects of the firing of cannons, several members of the audience panicked because they thought the theater was being bombed.[154]

• Two Italian laryngologists subjected Italian baritone Titta Ruffo to a number of scientific tests to determine the source of his magnificent voice. Scientific investigation can be painful. While connected to some scientific apparati, Mr. Ruffo hit a high A flat that made the scientists leave the room screaming because of aching teeth.[155]

• Writing a comic strip that appears in foreign newspapers does have disadvantages. Rudolph Dirks, who drew the comic-strip *The Katzenjammer Kids*, invented a character that spoke in rhyme. Unfortunately, this drove the person who translated the dialogue into Spanish crazy, and so Mr. Dirks dropped the character.[156]

• Ballet dancers may tend to stub their toes more often than other people because they aren't accustomed to looking down at the ground. According to Alexandra Danilova, the proper look for a ballet dancer is a "little bit snooty" — ballet dancers should have a slight upward tilt of the head.[157]

• In the mid-1950s, Gene Bozzacco, who was a musician with the Metropolitan Opera, remembered a funny performance of *Forza* in Brooklyn. Both men about to have a duel forgot their pistols, and they were forced to run off the stage in different directions to get them.[158]

• In the midst of a ballet, a wigpiece worn by ballerina Karen Kain flew off and landed on stage. Because the wigpiece was small and grey, it looked like a mouse, causing the members of the corps de ballet great perturbation.[159]

• Soon after John Barbirolli was knighted, opera/lieder singer Kathleen Ferrier made a charming mistake in addressing him. Instead of addressing him as "Sir John," she simply said, "Hello, luv."[160]

Chapter 4: From Money to Problem-Solving

Money

• Charles Dana Gibson received a lot of money for his illustrations. He once received a letter from a car company, which stated, "You are cordially invited to participate in our grand $100 prize contest. Each participant may submit one or more drawings advertising our automobile. The winner will receive a grand cash prize of $100. Drawings must be sent prepaid, and must be original, and all unsuccessful drawings will remain the property of the undersigned." Mr. Gibson received much more than $100 for one of his drawings, so this contest was laughable to him. He wrote this letter in reply to the car company: "You are cordially invited to participate in my grand $10 automobile contest. Each participant may submit one or more automobiles and the winner will receive a grand prize of $10. The automobiles submitted must be brand new and shipped [at your cost to] New York. They must be fully equipped. The unsuccessful automobiles will remain the property of the undersigned. Charles Dana Gibson."[161]

• Soprano Emma Eames was often asked to sing at benefits, and occasionally she got annoyed at society ladies who expected much for charity from her but little from themselves. She once made a proposal to some such society ladies who asked her to perform free at a benefit concert: "I will, on one condition. You are all wealthy ladies, far wealthier than I. Now, my usual [fee for singing] is £300. I will contribute that by singing, on condition that each of you will sign for the same amount." The society ladies said that they would think about it, and they did not bother her again. Music critic Henry T. Finck, a friend to Ms. Eames, wrote in *My Adventures in the Golden Age of Music*, his autobiography, "The charity of society women too often resembles Mark Twain's climbing of the Swiss mountains — by proxy." Ms. Eames was an independent spirit who was not afraid of offending people. She once said to Mr. Finck's wife, "I love to give parties for the pleasure of leaving out certain persons who want to come."[162]

• United States painter and teacher William M. Chase knew art. A Congressman who did not know art went around telling people about a bad painting that he owned, "Isn't that grand? A great bargain, too. Got it for four hundred dollars, and William M. Chase says it is worth ten thousand dollars." A friend of the painter heard what the Congressman had said, and the friend asked Mr. Chase about it. Mr. Chase explained, "He cornered me one day and wanted me to fix a value on it, but I told him I couldn't do it. He then came at me with a question I couldn't dodge: 'Well, Mr. Chase, how much would you charge to paint a picture like that?' I assured him most honestly that I wouldn't paint one like it for ten thousand dollars."[163]

• Soprano Kirsten Flagstad was good friends with her accompanist, Edwin McArthur, and often relied on him when she needed help. Following World War II, she left Norway and journeyed to Sweden, but she was not allowed to take much money with her. From the Carlton Hotel in Stockholm, she cabled Mr. McArthur, "I Am Here Without Funds. Please Do Something." Fortunately, Mr. McArthur was able to arrange for her to receive money. By the way, the first time Ms. Flagstad heard *Tristan und Isolde*, she was very bored and could barely keep awake. Later, she became famous for her singing of Wagnerian roles, including the role of Isolde.[164]

• John Phillip Sousa had a very difficult time selling his first composition. He trudged from one music company to another hoping to make a sale, but had no success. Finally, he made up his mind to either make a sale at the next music company, or give up entirely. He went inside, made his pitch to sell the composition for $25, but the manager said he would not pay 25 cents for it. Ready to give up, Mr. Sousa turned to leave, then noticed several dictionaries by the door.

He asked the manager, "Will you give me a dictionary for it?" The manager was willing, and so Mr. Sousa sold his first composition for a dictionary.[165]

• At the sale of the pictures that belonged to Henri Rouart, a journalist asked artist Edgar Degas, "Do you know how much your picture of two dancers at the bar, with a watering can, just sold for?" Mr. Degas replied, "No, I don't." The journalist told him the very high figure: 475,000 francs! Mr. Degas admitted, "That *is* a nice price." The journalist then asked, "Don't you think it outrageous that this picture will never bring you more than the five hundred francs you were paid for it?" Mr. Degas replied, "Monsieur, I am like the racehorse that wins the Grand Prize: I am satisfied with my ration of oats."[166]

• While he was still in high school, Navajo artist R.C. Gorman left several of his paintings at a trading post in Gallup, New Mexico, where he hoped they would be sold and he would make some money. After the summer was over, he returned to the trading post to see if the paintings had sold. The paintings had sold, all right, but when Mr. Gorman asked for his money, the white woman who ran the trading post told Mr. Gorman, "What money?" She then added, "I don't know you." Because Mr. Gorman didn't have a written contract, he didn't receive any money from the white woman.[167]

• William Gladstone once saw a portrait of a nobleman that he liked immensely but which he could not afford to buy. A few weeks after seeing the portrait, he was invited to a house to dine, where he saw the portrait hanging on the wall. Noticing Gladstone's interest in the portrait, his host said, "One of my ancestors." Gladstone replied, "If the portrait had cost less, he would have become one of my ancestors."[168]

• Science fiction writer Ray Bradbury loved theater and produced several of his own plays. He did not make money doing this. When his wife was still alive, every few years he would say to her, "Is this the year we open the window and throw the money out?" She would ask, "You want to do another play?" After he replied, "Yeah," she would say,

"Open the window." Mr. Bradbury said, "When I do a play, I throw the money out and it never comes back. And I don't expect it to."[169]

• Igor Stravinsky once met Mrs. Vera Newman at a party, and he started kissing her hand. Suddenly, he dropped her hand and said, "Oh, I forgot — your husband doesn't like my music." By the way, some people felt that Igor Stravinsky charged very high prices for his music. He once explained why: "I do it on behalf of my brother composers, Schubert and Mozart, who died in poverty."[170]

• Père Tanguy owned a store frequented by artists, some of whom paid for their paints with works of art. After Vincent van Gogh died, Mr. Tanguy sold one of Mr. van Gogh's still lifes for 42 francs. Asked why he had asked for that exact amount for the painting, Mr. Tanguy replied, "I looked up what poor van Gogh owed me when he died. It was 42 francs. Now I have got it back."[171]

• George Balanchine wanted a china silk curtain for his ballet *Orpheus* because it was beautiful and billowing. Unfortunately, it cost $1,000, and the ballet company didn't have it. Therefore, Mr. Balanchine disappeared for two hours, and then he came back with the money in cash. When asked where the money had come from, he replied only that he had not robbed a bank.[172]

• John Cage was usually a prolific composer, whether working with Merce Cunningham or on his own; however, Gordon Mumma, a composer for Mr. Cunningham, once noticed that Mr. Cage didn't compose any music in 1964 and asked him why. Mr. Cage explained that he was too busy to compose that year because of writing letters to raise funds for Merce Cunningham dance tours.[173]

• Pablo Picasso became very famous and very rich, and in his old age he didn't care about money. When he died, his heirs went through his belongings. They discovered a box of gold coins that he had apparently forgotten, and in drawers and cupboards, they discovered bundles of banknotes.[174]

• Oxford University once offered George Frideric Handel, composer of *Messiah*, an honorary doctorate. He was very pleased — until he found out that Oxford University was going to charge him £100 for the privilege. Handel decided to remain "Mr." instead of becoming "Dr."[175]

• In 1957, dancer Anton Dolin had supper with opera singer Maria Callas at the Café de Paris. After they had dined, Ms. Callas told Mr. Dolin why she had chosen that particular supper club: "I was offered £1,000 a week to come here and sing."[176]

• Georgia O'Keeffe once offered *Summer Days* to a museum for the price of $400,000, but the museum was reluctant to pay that price. No problem. She sold *Summer Days* to fashion designer Calvin Klein for $1 million.[177]

• Canadian painter Jean-Paul Piopelle once grew annoyed because art dealers priced his paintings by the number of square inches in them. Therefore, he created a circular painting to confuse them.[178]

• Early in his career as a painter, Claude Monet suffered from great poverty. Once, a laundress kept the Monet family sheets because he could not afford to pay his laundry bill.[179]

Movies

• When John Huston directed *Beat the Devil* (1954), he tore up the script, then invited Truman Capote to write new scenes. (During the filming, Mr. Capote spoke on the telephone each day to a pet raven. Once, when the pet raven declined to make any sounds on the telephone, Mr. Capote flew to Rome to see the raven in person.) In addition, Mr. Huston let the supporting actors — including, and especially, Peter Lorre and Robert Morley — make up their own dialogue. The movie flopped, but later it became a cult classic. As you would expect, Mr. Huston would have preferred that the movie be a success from day one. He said in 1975, "Of course it's about as bad to be ahead of your time as behind it. It's always nice when pictures are revived years later, it gives you the satisfaction of seeing them finally accepted, and God knows *Beat the Devil* and *The Asphalt Jungle* were no great shakes their first time around. But as far as the, ah, material rewards are concerned, it's better to have a success from the first."[180]

• In the movie *The Red Shoes*, starring Moira Shearer, Léonide Massine played the Shoemaker. As a result of the movie, he received more publicity than he had ever received. After making the movie, Mr. Massine vacationed in Italy, and a real shoemaker in Positano told him that he was ready to take him on as an assistant.[181]

Music and Musicians

• Choreography Hermes Pan once needed to work out a dance to some music by George Gershwin. He asked the rehearsal pianist in the studio to play the song, but was dissatisfied with it, so he asked the pianist to play the song at a slower tempo. Again, he was dissatisfied, and he said, "Gershwin or no Gershwin, I think this stinks!" Later that day, Mr. Pan was able to meet Mr. Gershwin and discovered he was the pianist at the rehearsal. Mr. Pan apologized to him, but Mr. Gershwin replied, "You know something? You might be right!"[182]

• Billy Rose once tried to impress choreographer Agnes de Mille with his plans for an arts production. Among other things, he asked what she would think if Leopold Stokowski came out in his theater and conducted a symphony orchestra in Debussy's "Claire de Lune." Ms. de Mille replied that she would be surprised, as no doubt would Mr. Stokowski, since "Claire de Lune" was written for solo piano, not for a symphony orchestra.[183]

• Sometimes symphony musicians don't like the new music they are playing. At a rehearsal for the premiere of Claude Debussy's *La Mer*, the musicians grew bored with the music. One of the musicians took the score, made a paper boat of it, then used his foot to push it along the floor. Soon many other musicians followed suit.[184]

Names

• Being famous under a pseudonym can lead to problems. Eric Blair, aka George Orwell, once learned that Ernest Hemingway was staying in a room at the same hotel he was staying at. He knocked on Mr. Hemingway's door and introduced himself as Eric Blair, and Mr. Hemingway asked what he wanted. Mr. Blair then reintroduced himself as George Orwell, and Mr. Hemingway said, "Why didn't you say so?" Then he invited him in for a drink. Mr. Blair could have told Mr. Hemingway about some odd experiences. For example, Mr. Orwell once rented a room from a landlady who was proud because she had worked for a nobleman. She was so proud that when she locked herself out of her house, she would not let her husband and Mr. Blair go next door to borrow a ladder to get to a high window and enter the house because she was too proud to associate with the neighbors. Instead, her husband and Mr. Blair walked a mile and borrowed a ladder from one of her relatives. And while working as a dishwasher and a porter in a Paris hotel, he was once ordered to get a single peach because a rich customer had ordered one. Since the hotel did not have a peach on the premises, Mr. Blair was ordered to find one or be fired. The shops were closed, but he found a basket of peaches hanging in a window. Rather than lose his job, he broke the window and stole one peach.[185]

• For a performance by ballerina Maria Tallchief and the New York City Ballet, Japanese stagehands waxed the stage floor. Of course, this resulted in dancers slipping, sliding, and falling. After that one ruinous performance, the stage floor was restored to its usual scuffed lack of splendor. By the way, at birth, Maria Tallchief's name was Elizabeth Marie Tall Chief. She changed "Tall Chief" to "Tallchief" because she wanted to avoid problems in alphabetization at school — other students wondered whether her last name was "Chief" or "Tall Chief." Her parents called her "Betty Marie," but when famed choreographer Agnes de Mille suggested that the world of ballet already had lots of Bettys and Elizabeths, Ms. Tallchief began to use the name "Maria" instead.[186]

• The first performance of George Frideric Handel's *Messiah* took place 23 April 1742, at Neal's Music Hall, located on Fishamble Street in Dublin. For this performance 700 people crowded into a space that was designed to hold only 600. The organizers of the concert realized that it would be crowded, so they bought newspaper advertisements asking gentlemen to leave their swords at home and asking women not to wear hoop skirts. By the way, the name "Fishamble" is interesting. A market used to be called a "shamble," and Neal's Music Hall used to be a fish market.[187]

• Agnes de Mille was determined to succeed as a dancer. Once, another dancer accidentally kicked her and broke her nose during a performance. Ms. de Mille continued dancing. By the way, while rehearsing her ballet *Rodeo*, choreographer and dancer Agnes de Mille worried about details. Eventually, the dancers working with her changed her name from "Agnes" to "Agonize." On 16 October 1942, *Rodeo* premiered with Ms. De Mille dancing the lead role of the Cowgirl. She was sure that the ballet had been a failure, but after taking 22 curtain calls, she finally believed that the premiere had been a success.[188]

• When the famous architect Frank Lloyd Wright was born in 1867, he was named Frank Lincoln Wright in honor of the recently assassinated President Abraham Lincoln. He changed his name after his parents divorced, and he took his new middle name from his mother, Anna Lloyd Jones.[189]

Opera

• Whenever Enrico Caruso performed, ovations greeted him. Therefore, he decided to perform an experiment to see if the audience would applaud him if they were unaware he was singing. He went to Albert Reiss, who was scheduled to sing an aria offstage in *Pagliacci*, and he arranged to sing the aria in Mr. Reiss' place. Unfortunately, Mr. Caruso received no applause, and no music critic noticed that Mr. Reiss had suddenly acquired a glorious voice. Mr. Caruso sadly noted, "It is not Caruso they want — it is only the knowledge that they are hearing Caruso!" By the way, Mr. Caruso sang with great power. When he performed Lucia for the first time at the Metropolitan Opera, Mr. Caruso sang with such force that a police officer showed up to find out where all the sound was coming from. Mr. Caruso said, "Aha! I sing too loud! I must look out for that."[190]

• Opera singers have very powerful voices. While in Paris, Gioacchino Rossini heard two powerful singers performing together. He wrote to a friend of his in Italy: "Lablache and Tamburini sang the duet from Bellini's *I Puritani*. I need not tell you anything about their performance. You surely heard it for yourself."[191]

• Christoph Willibald Gluck revolutionized opera. His controversial style caused much excitement in his opera *Armide*, whose premiere was packed. An usher requested one man in the audience to take off his hat, but the man replied, "You take it off; it's so crowded here that I can't move my arms."[192]

Poets

• As you may expect, Chilean poet Pablo Neruda, winner of the 1971 Nobel Prize for Literature, loved nature. As a boy, he and other boys engaged in fights in which they pelted each other with acorns. Sometimes, he would closely examine the color and shape of an acorn — an examination that was interrupted when the other boys pelted him with large numbers of acorns. People loved him and his poetry, which has been translated into many different languages. When Mr. Neruda was in political exile from Chili in 1949, he went to Europe and artist Pablo Picasso helped him get permission to stay in France. Mr. Neruda said, "He spoke to the authorities; he called up a good many people. I don't know how many marvelous paintings he failed to paint on account of me." On 11 April 1957, Mr. Neruda was arrested in Argentina because of his Communist leanings and put in jail for one and a half days. When he was released, one of his jailors gave him a gift. Mr. Neruda said, "I was about to leave the prison when one of the uniformed guards came up to me and put a sheet of paper in my hands. It was a poem he had dedicated to me. ... I imagine few poets have received a poetic homage from the men assigned to guard them." Also, he was delighted in May 1967, when he attended the Congress of Soviet Writers in Moscow and a floor-polisher saw him and recited from memory one of Mr. Neruda's poems. Of course, Mr. Neruda loved books and was influenced by such poets as Walt Whitman. As a recognized poet, he kept a photo of the bearded American poet on his desk at Isla Negra (Dark Island). A workman once looked at the photo and asked Mr. Neruda if the photo depicted his grandfather. Mr. Neruda replied, "Yes."[193]

• At age 23 Langston Hughes was both an undiscovered poet and an employed busboy. He worked in the restaurant of the Wardman Park Hotel in Washington, D.C., and he knew that famous poet Vachel Lindsay would be reading his poetry at the hotel. As an African-American in those Jim Crow days, Mr. Hughes knew that he could not attend the whites-only poetry reading, but he hoped to see Mr. Lindsay. When Mr. Lindsay and his wife sat down in the hotel restaurant to eat, Mr. Hughes approached their table and left three poems there. He wrote later, "Quickly, I laid them beside his plate and went away, afraid to say anything to so famous a poet, except to tell him I liked his poems and that these were poems of mine." Mr. Lindsay liked the poems, and at his poetry reading he announced that he had discovered a new and promising young poet, and he read all three of Mr. Hughes' poems. The next morning, Mr. Hughes was interviewed and photographed by newspaper employees. Mr. Lindsay also gave the young poet a gift: a set of books by Amy Lowell, along with the recommendation to study her poems. Later, Mr. Hughes wrote about Mr. Lindsay, "He was a great, kind man. And he is one of the people I remember with pleasure and gratitude out of my bewildered days in Washington."[194]

Prejudice

• When African-American jazz musician Louis Armstrong was a little boy, he learned about the Jim Crow laws in New Orleans. One day, he got on a streetcar, and he sat in a front seat, not knowing that the streetcar was segregated and that black passengers were supposed to sit in the back. A white woman told him to sit in the back, but young Louis simply made faces at her. Angry, the white woman stood up, grabbed Louis, and hauled him to one of the seats in the back of the bus. By the way, early in his career, Mr. Armstrong was riding in a car through New York City's Central Park when the radiator cap blew off. Immediately, police officers surrounded the automobile and searched its African-American passengers to see if they were carrying firearms. Of course, not everyone is prejudiced. Mr. Armstrong was friends with white jazz trombonist Jack Teagarden, who once told him in the slang of the time, "You a spade and I'm an ofay. We got the same soul. Let's blow." By the way, as a very young boy, Louis wanted to learn to play the cornet, but he didn't have enough money to buy one. Fortunately, a Russian Jewish immigrant family he worked for, the Karnofskys, loaned him the money to buy a cornet. This is fortunate because Mr. Armstrong was very influential; he blazed a path for so many other jazz musicians. Dizzy Gillespie once said about Mr. Armstrong, "No him, no me."[195]

• The great black dancer Bill Robinson, aka Mr. Bojangles, once was in an all-night diner at 4 a.m. He ordered a meal, but the server told him, "We don't serve your kind." Mr. Bojangles took out his gun, laid it on the table, then gave his order again. This time he was served, but after eating he was arrested by a rookie deputy. However, he was immediately released because he was a friend of the sheriff. Mr. Bojangles always took steps to become friendly with police officers in every town he played. His wife was also very good at public relations, writing the chief of police in each town her husband played to give warm wishes to the chief's wife and to give them free tickets to the show. By the way, Mr. Bojangles had a serious weakness for vanilla ice cream, and reportedly ate four to eight quarts per day.[196]

• Benny Goodman, a white, Jewish jazz musician, formed the Benny Goodman Trio. The group consisted of himself, drummer Gene Krupa, and pianist Teddy Wilson. In addition to creating excellent jazz, the group represented a major step forward in race relations because Mr. Wilson was black. Previously, white and black musicians had not played together in public. At the time the group was formed, the 1930s, racism was prevalent in the United States. For example, in 1931, Earl Hines and the members of his jazz band were not allowed to walk on the sidewalks in Fort Lauderdale, Florida, because they were black. They had no choice but to walk in the streets.[197]

Problem-Solving

• Arturo Toscanini had poor eyesight — he memorized his scores so that he didn't need to refer to them during performances or rehearsals. He once wanted perfection in the tinkling of some very small antique cymbals to be used in Berlioz' "Queen Mab" scherzo. Several musicians failed to meet Toscanini's standards, so Sam Borodkin — who played such instruments as the bass drum, glockenspiel, tam-tam, and gong — said that he would try to do it. Mr. Borodkin succeeded brilliantly — but through the use of a trick. Instead of using two antique cymbals and hitting them against each other, he used a metal triangle stick and hit it against one antique cymbal. Because Toscanini had such poor eyesight, and because Mr. Borodkin was bent over his music stand, hiding the metal triangle stick, the trick succeeded in fooling Maestro Toscanini. By the way, someone was amazed at Maestro Toscanini's phenomenal memory — as demonstrated by his conducting without a score in front of him — and asked, "Tell me, maestro, how do you learn all those scores from memory?" Toscanini replied brusquely, "I learn them."[198]

• Ron Galella is the perhaps most famous of all paparazzi, aka celebrity photographers. Marlon Brando once punched him, knocking out five teeth. After being treated at an emergency room and having his jaw wired, Mr. Galella went back to get more photographs of Mr.

Brando. The next time that Mr. Galella wanted to photograph Mr. Brando, Mr. Gallela was wearing a football helmet for protection. While making the movie *Three Days of the Condor*, actor Robert Redford wanted to avoid being photographed by Mr. Galello. While at *The New York Times* building, Mr. Redford — in the words of Roger Ebert, who respects the tenacity of Mr. Galello — "entered one end of the building, raced through its second floor to the other end, slipped into his trailer, disguised his stand-in as a double, and had him run to his car and be driven away." From a safe distance, Mr. Redford was able to watch Mr. Galello jump onto the trunk of the limo to snap a photograph through the back window.[199]

• In Thomas Beecham's early years, England had many choir masters with perfect ears but limited music education. Nevertheless, they could make the choir sing — and sing well. Mr. Beecham knew of one case where an elderly composer was asked to conduct his own music, but unfortunately arrived in the town too late to rehearse with the choir before the concert. At the concert, the composer began to conduct the music at a tempo much slower than the choir had rehearsed it, with the result being musical chaos. The choir master, horrified, shouted, "Take no notice of him [the conductor] — sing it as you've learned it." The choir came together, sang mightily and well — and the orchestra and conductor were forced to go along with the choir's tempo.[200]

• Alicia Markova's father died when she was very young, leaving the family destitute. Her friend Anton Dolin wanted her to dance with Sergei Diaghilev's dance company, but Mr. Diaghilev would not hear of it, in part because he was not interested in child prodigies and in part because he was displeased over publicity that the dancers in his company were British. (Mr. Diaghilev changed their names when they joined his company. Anton Dolin's real name was Patrick Kay, and Alicia Markova's real name was Alicia Marks.) Therefore, Mr. Dolin and Ms. Markova's dance teacher Seraphine Astafieva arranged an audition by trickery. They invited Mr. Diaghilev to a party at which Ms. Markova entertained by dancing. Mr. Diaghilev was astounded by what he saw, and he invited her to join his dance company.[201]

• From 1948-1957, the New York City Ballet was based at City Center. During all that time, NYCB founders George Balanchine and Lincoln Kirstein never drew a salary. Instead, when they needed money, they found it elsewhere. For example, Mr. Balanchine would make money on Broadway or by staging a ballet for another dance company. When Lincoln Center was built, American ballet master Mr. Balanchine wanted it to be perfect. After learning that the orchestra pit would hold only 35 musicians, he was furious — until his wishes were heeded, and some already-poured concrete was jackhammered into pieces in order to double the size of the orchestra pit.[202]

• Ballet dancers have tricks to make them forget how much their feet hurt. During a ballet class, David Howard once told Leslie Browne while she was doing a series of pirouettes, "This is where you imagine you have a huge piece of gum in your mouth and you push it against the roof of your mouth with your tongue as hard as you can, hoping to push the gum through." Ms. Browne was confused by this comment, until Mr. Howard told her, "Then you will forget how much your feet hurt."[203]

• Enrico Caruso was a strong believer in personal hygiene. Once, he and his wife accepted an invitation to sit in the box of a French tenor. However, after he was seated, Mr. Caruso turned to his host and said, "Monsieur, Madame cannot remain unless you go home and brush your teeth." The French tenor went home and brushed his teeth. By the way, according to Mr. Caruso's wife, Dorothy, in the course of each performance he lost three pounds.[204]

• While in Milan to direct *The Nutcracker* near the end of his career, Rudolf Nureyev handled an ultimatum by a principal dancer with finesse. As Mr. Nureyev was walking away from the set, the principal dancer said that she would not dance on opening night unless her boyfriend also had a leading part. Still walking, Mr. Nureyev ordered that another principal dancer be found to take her place. The ballerina immediately retracted her ultimatum.[205]

• Opera singer Grace Moore often answered her own telephone; however, being a celebrity, she disguised her voice with a French accent until she learned who the caller was. Sometimes, she was unable to identify important callers and so would not speak to them. Discovering the truth later, they were not amused at the precaution she had taken to preserve her privacy.[206]

• John "Trane" Coltrane used to play long saxophone solos, and once he told Miles Davis that he didn't know how to stop. Mr. Davis replied, "Try taking the saxophone out of your mouth." By the way, jazz musician Dizzy Gillespie started out playing the trombone as a kid, but he quickly switched to trumpet — he couldn't play all the notes on the trombone because his arms were too short.[207]

• As a young boy, ballet student Alexander Godunov was short, even considering his age. After being told that tomato juice would make him grow, he began to drink gallons of it. He also heard that sleeping on a soft bed would keep him short, so he began to sleep on boards. Something worked — he grew to be over six feet tall.[208]

• Even people who don't like classical music like Gioacchino Rossini's "Overture" to *William Tell* because it is the theme music of the Lone Ranger. According to Rossini, he wrote the music at a furious pace in an apartment on the Boulevard Montmartre in Paris because he was trying to block the noisy street from his mind.[209]

• George Frideric Handel once had trouble with Francesca Cuzzoni, one of the singers in his opera *Ottone*. Being quite strong, Handel picked up Ms. Cuzzoni and held her out a window, two stories above the street, and threatened to drop her. Ms. Cuzzoni decided to sing her part the way Mr. Handel wanted her to.[210]

• Conductor Claudio Abbado has an interesting way of dealing with an orchestra whose members speak too loudly during rehearsals.

He speaks softer and softer and finally stops speaking entirely. At that point, the members of the orchestra realize that they need to be quiet in order for the rehearsal to proceed.[211]

• Choreographer George Balanchine was remarkably unperturbed during crises. In 1954, shortly before the premiere of his *Nutcracker* ballet, he learned that the costumes weren't ready. Therefore, he picked up a needle and a costume and started sewing along with the seamstresses.[212]

• Colonel W. de Basil sometimes insisted that he be photographed although the newspaper photographer really wanted only photographs of the Colonel's ballet troupe. In such cases, the photographer pretended to photograph the Colonel — but there wasn't any film in the camera.[213]

• Tony Baines, a bassoonist for the London Philharmonic Orchestra, once made the error of showing up for the ballet in tails rather than black tie. No problem. He simply dipped his tie in black ink. Of course, it dripped all over his shirt, but he declined to let that bother him.[214]

• John Christie was a very rich man. While listening to a musical performance in a very hot theater (in the days before air conditioning), he grew very uncomfortable, so he used scissors to cut off the sleeves of his shirt and dress jacket.[215]

• Fans once surrounded Pablo Picasso at a time when he did not want to be surrounded by fans. No problem. He took out a gun he had with him and fired it into the air, and very quickly he was no longer surrounded by fans.[216]

• American dance pioneer Ted Shawn came up with an original way to stop obesity in the United States. Simply require everyone to stand for one hour per year naked in public — vanity would soon make obesity vanish.[217]

Chapter 5: From Respect to Work

Respect

• Alexandra Danilova was asked about the difference between a very good ballet dancer (a soloist) and a ballerina (of course, not every woman ballet dancer is a ballerina — only the very best are). She replied, "Ballet is *Giselle*. Door of cottage open. Pretty young soloist comes out. You happy and say 'I hope she do well.' Another performance. Is also *Giselle*. Alicia Markova come out. She not danced yet. One step only, but you sigh and say, 'Ah! ballerina!' You do not ask, you know. She is star. She shine."[218]

• Suzanne Farrell was a great admirer of ballerina Diana Adams. Once, Ms. Adams gave her a pin of a mouse with painted whiskers and a long tail. Thereafter, Ms. Farrell pinned the mouse — despite its scratchy tail — inside her bra for good luck at important ballets. In addition, Ms. Farrell named her diary, to which she confided her inmost thoughts, "Diana."[219]

Stage Fright

• Greek-American soprano Maria Callas suffered terribly from stage fright before giving a performance. Before performances, Ms. Callas used to hold onto the arm of someone in the wings. Her dresser once displayed her arm to Sir John Tooley — it was bruised from the wrist to the elbow. Once, Ms. Callas' fingernails drew blood from another supporter's hand.[220]

• Famous pianist Adolphe Henselt suffered so badly from stage fright that he used to stay offstage until the very last minute, then rush onstage to play his solo before running offstage again. Once, he had to rush so quickly to the piano that he wasn't able to put out his cigar first, so he had to smoke throughout his solo.[221]

Travel

• Fashion designer Vicky Tiel tends to dress comfortably for flights, as do many people of wealth and fashion. For one flight, she wore ripped jeans and a ripped jean jacket. She had a boarding pass for first class, but the stewardess looked her over and made her sit in coach, although she protested. She says, "Didn't the hostess know that the antitravel look is for those who *really* travel? The well-dressed couple in first class is actually the pretty secretary sleeping with her older boss, hoping to move up to trophy wife." When she arrived in Atlanta, she wanted to file a complaint, but Leticia Moise from CNN Atlanta recognized her and suggested a story: "The Fashion Designer Who was Thrown Out of First Class." Ms. Tiel modeled the clothing she was wearing, and Ms. Moise asked a passerby, "Would you let her into first class?" He looked her over, and then he said into the microphone, "H*ll, no!"[222]

• Cellist Pablo Casals was born and grew up in Catalonia. While on tour in the United States, he visited the territory of New Mexico. While walking in the desert, Mr. Casals and pianist Léon Moreau came across a cabin. The cabin's owner, who was dressed like a cowboy, greeted them. Mr. Casals noticed his accent, and he asked the man where he was from. "It's a country you never heard of," the man said. "Catalonia." Mr. Casals enjoyed seeing and learning new things. To understand the life of coal miners in the United States, Mr. Casals and Mr. Moreau went down into a mineshaft in Wilkes-Barre, Pennsylvania. When Mr. Casals and Mr. Moreau reached the surface again, it was time for their concert, which they gave while still covered with coal dust.[223]

• Despite being born in Boston, George Copeland played Spanish music very well and even lived in Spain; however, he abandoned his Spanish villa just before a revolutionary war broke out. He had a good reason. One morning, he discovered one of his Loyalist servants on the patio. More specifically, he found the servant's head — the rest of the servant was nowhere to be found.[224]

• When choreographer Anthony Tudor first came to the United States, he arrived on Columbus Day. All the banks were closed and no bonds had been posted, so he was forced to remain on Ellis Island that night. Fortunately, he enjoyed the company he found there.[225]

War

• Some people have the money but not necessarily the intelligence to attend significant musical events. A truly intelligent pianist, Denis Matthews, once overheard this during a program conducted by Arturo Toscanini: "When is Toscanini coming on? Don't tell me he is only the conductor!" By the way, Mr. Matthews played piano for the British armed forces during World War II. During a blackout, an old woman saw him and some other musicians. She saw that they were wearing uniforms, and supposing that the instruments many of the musicians were holding were lethal weapons of war, told them, "That's right, lads — give them hell!"[226]

• When opera singer Maria Callas was a young girl, she sometimes got caught lying, so her mother used to punish her in accordance with an old Greek custom — she put pepper on young Maria's lips. By the way, Maria's Uncle Filon was a saboteur for the Greeks during World War II. He worked as an engineer at an air base for the Nazis, and he managed to destroy nine German airplanes by putting sugar in their gas tanks. The Nazis discovered what he was doing, so he had to flee for his life. After the war, the Communists who tried to take over Greece killed him.[227]

• To protest war, artist David Smith created a series of Medals for Dishonor — bronze medallions with anti-war imagery. Because the public supported World War II, it disliked the medallions, but that didn't bother Mr. Smith: "Never sold a one. But I would rather have the approval of other artists and critics than monetary sales reward."[228]

Weight

• When Simon Doonan, the world-famous window dresser at Barney's in New York, began aerobics, one of his fellow enthusiasts was a reporter for the *National Enquirer*, and she constantly asked him if he had any dirt on celebrities. He never did, but actress Shelley Winters came into Barney's one day, and he saw her buy a pair of leather pants — size six. Ms. Winters is a wonderful actress, of course, but she is not a size six. The leather pants were not a gift, and she was not planning on wearing them; instead, she was planning on hanging them on her refrigerator door as a reminder of why she wanted to lose weight: to fit into size-six leather pants. At his next aerobics class, Mr. Doonan told the *National Enquirer* reporter what he had witnessed, and she took notes. Soon an item about Ms. Winters and her size-six leather pants appeared in the *National Enquirer*, and soon a check for $50 arrived in Mr. Doonan's mailbox with the notation "for Shelley Winters item." Mr. Doonan felt guilty, and he wondered if he had betrayed Ms. Winters. But the next day, some designer aerobics wear arrived at Barney's. Among the items was a pair of cycle shorts by Stephen Sprouse. They were orange, black, and white, and they cost $50. Mr. Doonan bought the cycle shorts and stopped feeling guilty. He says, "I was the talk of my aerobics class that night."[229]

• Anton Dolin once danced with Alexandra Danilova at a time when she was overweight. After he had lifted her several times in the *Blue Bird pas de deux*, he complained to her, "I am a dancer — *not* a porter!" Ms. Danilova began dieting immediately.[230]

Wit

• The Guerilla Girls engage in activism for artists who are women or people of color. They wear gorilla masks and are anonymous, taking on the names of deceased famous women creators. Guerilla Girl "Frida Kahlo" once was out of costume and talking with some other people to art dealer Diane Brown. By them was a poster that the Guerilla Girls had put up. Diane's young son read the poster out loud: "Diane Brown [...] shows less than ten percent women artists or none at all." He then asked his mother, "What does that mean, Mommy?" She did not answer him, but later when she appeared in a CNN TV special titled

Gender Wars, she complained that the Guerilla Girls had attacked her because she showed less than fifty percent women artists. "Frida Kahlo" complains, "Math is *soooo* hard for women." By the way, Guerilla Girl "Käthy Kollwitz" was out of costume and talking to a male chief curator and his female assistant when the male chief curator turned to "Käthy Kollwitz" and said about his female assistant, "I think she's a Guerilla Girl." "Käthy Kollwitz" asked why he thought that, and he explained, "Because every time we propose a group show, or get an announcement from another museum, she always counts the number of women artists. Don't you think that's ridiculous?" Guerilla Girl "Käthy Kollwitz" replied, "Not at all. All women count."[231]

• People respond to music in different, but often witty, ways: 1) John Cage's 4'33" is a composition that can be performed by anyone any way he or she wishes as long as the performance takes exactly 4 minutes and 33 seconds. A notable performance of the piece involved a pianist sitting at a piano for exactly 4 minutes and 33 seconds without striking a single key. After hearing about this performance, Igor Stravinsky said that he wished to hear a full-length composition by Mr. Cage. 2) George Bernard Shaw once ate at a restaurant where a band played popular music. The proprietor of the restaurant brought him a card on which he could write what he wanted the band to play. Mr. Shaw wrote, "Dominoes."[232]

• Many people in ballet are witty: 1) Ballet dancer George Zoritch was once requested to give a speech, even if it were only two words long. Therefore, he stood up and said, "One! Two!" His speech was rewarded with laughter. 2) Ballet dancer Igor Youskevitch once told a beautiful waitress, "If I may be so bold, a martini is like a beautiful girl's bosom. One is not enough, but three is too many!" 3) Pavel Petroff had a dry wit as a Russian ballet teacher. Sometimes, he would tell some of the students in his class, "A ballerina you will never make, but a seamstress, perhaps!"[233]

• Many critics are witty: 1) Eugene d'Albert was asked to read and express his opinion of a piano concerto by German composer Max Vogrich. Mr. d'Albert looked at the concerto closely and then stated his opinion: "The ink and paper are excellent." By the way, an English lord became known as Lord Monday because he fell in love with German operatic soprano Henrietta Sontag and followed her the way that Monday follows Sunday. (*Sonntag* means Sunday.) 2) A critic wrote these puns in the 1870 *Musical Standard*: "We *hang* on every note Madame Sontag sings — / This proves the lady's great powers of *execution*."[234]

• Tom Waits has been a successful singer-songwriter for decades, but he is far from being a sell-out, in more ways than one. In her book *Tom Waits*, Cath Carroll includes a discography but does not include information about how high the songs or albums reached on the record charts. Mr. Carroll writes, " ... noting chart positions on a Tom Waits discography is like putting Barbie clothes on a bulldog." By the way, Mr. Waits can be witty. He once said, "She's been married so many times she's got rice marks all over her face."[235]

• Paul Beard used to lead the orchestra for Sir Thomas Beecham. Later, he led a different orchestra — the BBC Symphony Orchestra — upon which he stamped his personality and at which Sir Thomas was asked to be a guest conductor. At the end of a rehearsal, Sir Thomas stood in front of the orchestra, stroked his goatee, and said, "May I suggest to you, gentlemen, that when we reassemble, you pay a little more attention to *this* beard?"[236]

• Sir William S. Gilbert was funny in real life. Once, an obese lady attended one of his rehearsals. While his back was turned, she disappeared, so Sir William asked a stagehand where she had gone. The stagehand pointed to some scenery and said, "She's round behind." Sir William replied, "I asked you for her geography, not her description."[237]

Work

• Tarina Tarantino creates fashionable jewelry and is the head of her own company. Her hair is also fashionable: hot pink. She says, "I got married with pink hair. I had two babies with pink hair. And I'll be an old lady with pink hair." To make her particular color of hot pink, her hair stylist mixes four shades of colors. Why hot pink? She explains that she "wanted to experience a way of living through color." Once, a woman in a coffee shop said to her, "You must have a very tolerant boss to allow you to come to work with pink hair." Ms. Tarantino replied, "Actually, my boss has the same color hair." As the head of her company, she has to manage a staff of design assistants and factory workers. One young employee was unhappy with her performance review, so she asked Ms. Tarantino to speak to her mother. Ms. Tarantino replied, "Your mother doesn't work here." Her office and manufacturing facility is called the Sparkle Factory, and in 2011 it moved to another building on which the graffiti artist Banksy had received permission to paint an exterior wall. He painted a picture of a girl on a swing — the word "Parking" had been turned into "Park." Ms. Tarantino got her big break when actress Cameron Diaz wore a Tarantino bracelet to the 2002 Oscars. These days, Ms. Tarantino believes, movie stars all have consultants who tell them what to wear. These days, she says, her own big break "would never happen."[238]

• Like many writers, Carl Sandburg had a great wealth of experience from his childhood and his many jobs to draw upon for inspiration. As a young boy, he was arrested for skinny-dipping in a neighborhood pond. His parents thought that the arrest was silly; they had seen Carl naked when he was born, and they saw him naked whenever he took a bath in a laundry tub. Young Carl once got a summer job washing bottles from 7 a.m. to 6 p.m. in a bottling works. (This was before modern child-labor laws.) He was allowed to drink as much soda pop as he wanted, and he drank so much that he got diarrhea and lost his job. For a while, he rode the rails as a hobo. One night he and four other hoboes tried to sleep in an empty boxcar, but it was so cold that they gave up and walked to a jail where a kind sheriff let them sleep on the floor of a cell. When Carl attended college, he had a job as a firefighter. His professors knew that whenever the town's fire whistle blew, Carl had to leave class and fight a fire.[239]

• As a beginning cartoonist, Ted Rall wanted people to see his art. After meeting graffiti artist Keith Haring, he thought, "*He* has the approach." What is the approach? Instead of working to please editors, who are pleased by generic work, simply get your art in front of the people. Therefore, Ted took his cartoons, went to the bank he hated working at, and ran off 700 copies very early in the morning on the bank's Xerox machine. Then he and his girlfriend walked through Broadway, Harlem, and Times Square and pasted the cartoons wherever they could. The walking and pasting took four hours and covered seven miles. He put his PO address on the cartoons and got fan mail — and he got letters from editors who wrote, "I was visiting New York. I saw your cartoon on the wall and ripped it down. I was wondering if you'd mind if we ran your cartoons." Ted quit the bank job he hated and became a professional cartoonist.[240]

• Comic singer Anna Russell once worked in a pantomime at the Ashton Circus in Australia, which is as famous there as the Ringling Brothers Circus is in the United States. Most of the pantomime performers stayed in hotels, but Ms. Russell decided that she wanted to experience the circus life, so she rented a trailer and stayed with the circus performers. At the end of the season, she was presented with a medal that had her name on one side and the Ashton crest on the other. According to the ancient tradition of the circus, she could get a job — even if it is nothing more than washing the elephants — at any circus in the world simply by showing the circus her medal.[241]

• Régine Crespin, a woman of conviction, was supposed to sing the title role in *Tosca*, but during a rehearsal she sang a phrase faster than the conductor, Francesco Molinari-Pradelli, wanted her to sing it. He told her, "Signora, that phrase does not go that way." Very politely, she replied, "Maestro, if you don't mind, we can discuss these details afterward." Mr. Molinari-Pradelli then rudely said, "No, there is nothing to discuss. It will be done as I say, and that's that." This was too rude for Ms. Crespin, so she said, "*Tant pis*" [roughly, "So much for me working for you"], left, and Mr. Molinari-Pradelli was forced to find another person to sing the role of Tosca.[242]

• In 1948, Sir Thomas Beecham was scheduled to present a program of English music at the Royal Albert Hall, but few tickets were sold and he cancelled the concert. Sensing an opportunity, the Bournemouth Corporation immediately called him and asked him to present the same program using their orchestra in Bournemouth — and they guaranteed a full house. Sir Thomas accepted, and conducted in front of a full house, as promised. Playing celesta in the Bournemouth orchestra was Rudolph Schwarz, the regular conductor of the orchestra, who wanted the privilege of playing for Sir Thomas.[243]

• Duke Ellington played in a lot of places as a young jazz musician, including a club near Broadway that was supposed to be run by gangsters and that oddly kept catching on fire. Occasionally, the owner told Mr. Ellington and the other musicians that a certain night was a good night to take their musical instruments home because an "accident" was about to happen. By the way, Mr. Ellington understood the power of word-of-mouth advertising. When he was a young musician, he used to pay people to go around and tell other people how good he and his band were.[244]

• Walking through the Louvre, Paul Valéry and artist Edgar Degas saw a large painting of large oak trees by Henri Rousseau. Mr. Valéry admired the painting, and he marveled at how the artist had painted so many individual leaves. He said, "It is superb, but how tedious, painting all those leaves. What a dreadful bore that must have been." Mr. Degas responded, "Be still. Had it not been tedious, there would have been no enjoyment in it."[245]

• Mexican artist Diego Rivera put his art before everything else. Often, he worked 15 to 18 hours a day, every day of the week. He would snack rather than eat, and his common-law wife, Guadalupe Marín, once complained that he didn't stop working long enough even to take a bath. During 1932-1933, Mr. Rivera worked so hard painting murals that he lost 100 pounds![246]

No one ever thinks of ballerinas collecting unemployment insurance, but they do. During the off-season, when all the ballet dancers were laid off, ballerina Alice Patelson used to go downtown to the unemployment insurance office on 90th Street and Broadway, where she would see other dancers with the New York City Ballet.[247]

• Robert M. Brinkerhoff, the cartoonist of the long-ago comic strip *Little Mary Mixup*, had a yen for travel and a strong work ethic. The two worked well together. Before he traveled to the Orient, he turned in 100 cartoons to the United Feature Syndicate. For two years previously, he had created one extra cartoon each week.[248]

• While choreographing a new production of *Swan Lake*, Peter Wright told ballerina Galina Samsova, who was to be carried by the dancer playing Rothbart, that she had to be down the alley formed by two rows of swans in a very quick time. Ms. Samsova laughed, then said, "I'm easy — I'm being carried."[249]

• When New York City Ballet ballerina Wendy Whelan was asked what she liked least about her choice of careers, she replied, "The knowledge that it'll be over." (What she likes most are the people she works with.)[250]

Appendix A: Bibliography

Alda, Frances. *Men, Women, and Tenors*. Boston, MA: Houghton Mifflin Company, 1937.

Anecdotes of the Hour By Famous Men. New York: Hearst's International Library Company, 1914.

Anton Seidl: A Memorial by His Friends. New York: Charles Scribner's Sons, 1899.

Atkinson, Margaret F. and May Hillman. *Dancers of the Ballet*. New York: Alfred A. Knopf, 1955.

Augustyn, Frank, and Shelley Tanaka. *Footnotes: Dancing the World's Best-Loved Ballets*. Brookfield, CT: The Millbrook Press, 2001.

Ayre, Leslie. *The Wit of Music*. Boston, MA: Crescendo Publishing Company, 1969.

Baer, Nancy Van Norman. *Bronislava Nijinska: A Dancer's Legacy*. San Francisco, CA: Fine Arts Museums of San Francisco, 1986.

Barber, David W. *Bach, Beethoven, and the Boys*. Toronto, Canada: Sound and Vision, 1996.

Barber, David W. *Getting a Handel on Messiah*. Toronto, Canada: Sound and Vision, 1994.

Barnes, Clive. *Inside American Ballet Theatre*. New York: Hawthorn Books, 1977.

Beaumont, Cyril W. *Vaslav Nijinsky*. New York: Haskell House Publishers, 1974.

Beecham, Thomas. A *Mingled Chime*. New York: Da Capo Press, 1976.

Bing, Sir Rudolf. *5000 Nights at the Opera*. Garden City, NY: Doubleday and Company, Inc., 1972.

Boerst, William J. *Generous Anger: The Story of George Orwell*. Greensboro, NC: Morgan Reynolds, Inc., 2001.

Boerst, William J. *Isaac Asimov: Writer of the Future*. Greensboro, NC: Morgan Reynolds, Inc., 1999.

Borge, Victor, and Robert Sherman. *My Favorite Comedies in Music*. New York: Franklin Watts, 1980.

Borge, Victor, and Robert Sherman. *My Favorite Intermissions*. Garden City, NY: Doubleday and Co., Inc., 1971.

Boyden, John, collector. *Stick to the Music: Scores of Orchestral Tales*. London: Souvenir Press, 1992.

Brackett, Virginia. *A Home in the Heart: The Story of Sandra Cisneros*. Greensboro, NC: Morgan Reynolds Publishing, Inc., 2005.

Brubach, Holly. *Ten Dancers*. Photographs by Pierre Petitjean. New York: William Morrow and Company, Inc., 1982.

Callas, Evangelia. *My Daughter Maria Callas*. New York: Fleet Publishing Corporation, 1960.

Cardus, Neville, editor. *Kathleen Ferrier: A Memoir*. London: Hamish Hamilton, Ltd., 1954.

Carroll, Cath. *Tom Waits*. New York: Thunder's Mouth Press, 2000.

Caruso, Dorothy. *Enrico Caruso: His Life and Death*. New York: Simon and Schuster, Inc., 1945.

Chotzinoff, Samuel. *Toscanini: An Intimate Portrait*. New York: Alfred A. Knopf, 1956.

Cott, Ted. *The Victor Book of Musical Fun*. New York: Simon and Schuster, Inc., 1945.

Cubberley, William, and Joseph Carmen. *Round About the Ballet*. Photographs by Roy Round. Pompton Plains, NJ: Limelight Editions, 2004.

Danilova, Alexandra. *Choura: The Memoirs of Alexandra Danilova*. New York: Alfred A. Knopf, 1986.

Davis, Francis A. *Frank Lloyd Wright: Maverick Architect*. Minneapolis, MN: Lerner Publications Company, 1996.

de Mille, Agnes. *Portrait Gallery*. Boston, MA: Houghton Mifflin Company, 1990.

Dolin, Anton. *Alicia Markova: Her Life and Art*. New York: Hermitage House, 1953.

Domingo, Plácido. *My First Forty Years*. New York: Alfred A Knopf, 1983.

Doonan, Simon. *Confessions of a Window Dresser*. New York: Penguin Studio, 1998.

Doonan, Simon. *Eccentric Glamour*. New York: Simon and Schuster, 2008.

Douglas, Nigel. *More Legendary Voices*. London: Andre Deutsch Limited, 1994.

Drew, John. *My Years on the Stage*. New York: E.P. Dutton & Company, 1922.

Editors of Dance Magazine, with text by Gloria Manor. *The Gospel According to Dance*. New York: St. Martin's Press, 1980.

Ewen, David. *Dictators of the Baton*. Chicago, IL: Ziff-Davis Publishing Company, 1948.

Ewen, David. *Famous Modern Conductors*. New York: Dodd, Mead & Company, 1967.

Farrell, Suzanne. *Holding On to the Air*. New York: Summit Books, 1990.

Finck, Henry T. *My Adventures in the Golden Age of Music*. New York and London: Funk & Wagnalls Company, 1926.

Finck, Henry T. *Musical Laughs*. New York: Funk & Wagnalls Company, 1924.

Fonteyn, Margot. *Autobiography*. New York: Alfred A. Knopf, 1976.

Fonteyn, Margot, presenter. *Pavlova: Portrait of a Dancer*. New York: Viking Penguin Inc., 1984.

Ford, Carin T. *Legends of American Dance and Choreography*. Berkeley Heights, NJ: Enslow Publications, Inc., 2000.

Frank, Rusty E. *Tap! The Greatest Tap Dance Stars and Their Stories, 1900-1955*. New York: William Morrow and Company, Inc., 1990.

Franks, A.H., editor. *Pavlova: A Collection of Memoirs*. New York: Da Capo Press, Inc., 1956.

Furst, Herbert. *The New Anecdotes of Painters and Paintings*. London: The Bodley Head, Ltd., 1926.

Gale, Joseph. *Behind Barres: The Mystique of Masterly Teaching*. New York: Dance Horizons, 1980.

Garden, Mary, and Louis Biancolli. *Mary Garden's Story*. New York: Simon and Schuster, Inc., 1951.

Giles, Sarah. *Fred Astaire: His Friends Talk*. New York: Doubleday, 1988.

Gonzales, Doreen. *Diego Rivera: His Art, His Life*. Berkeley Heights, NJ: Enslow Publications, Inc., 1996.

Goodnough, David. *Pablo Casals: Cellist for the World*. Springfield, NJ: Enslow Publications, Inc., 1997.

Greenberg, Jan, and Sandra Jordan. *The American Eye: Eleven Artists of the Twentieth Century*. New York: Delacorte Press, 1995.

Greenberg, Jan, and Sandra Jordan. *Vincent van Gogh: Portrait of an Artist*. New York: Delacorte Press, 2001.

Gregory, Cynthia. *Cynthia Gregory Dances Swan Lake*. New York: Simon and Schuster, Inc., 1990.

Gregory, John, editor. *Heritage of a Ballet Master: Nicolas Legat*. London: Dance Books, Ltd., 1978.

Greskovic, Robert. *Ballet 101*. New York: Hyperion, 1998.

Groover, David L., and Cecil C. Conner, Jr. *Skeletons from the Opera Closet*. New York: St. Martin's Press, 1986.

Gruen, John. *People Who Dance*. Pennington, NJ: Princeton Book Company, 1988.

Guerrilla Girls. *Confessions of the Guerilla Girls*. New York: HarperPerennial, 1995.

Haskins, Jim, and N.R. Mitgang. *Mr. Bojangles: The Story of Bill Robinson*. New York: William Morrow and Company, Inc., 1988.

Hermann, Spring. *R.C. Gorman: Navaho Artist*. Springfield, NJ: Enslow Publications, Inc., 1995.

Hewlett-Davies, Barry, editor and compiler. *A Night at the Opera*. New York: St. Martin's Press, 1980.

Heylbut, Rose, and Aimé Gerber. *Backstage at the Opera*. New York: Thomas Y. Crowell Company, 1937.

Humphrey, Laning, compiler. *The Humor of Music and Other Oddities in the Art*. Boston, MA: Crescendo Publishing Company, 1971.

Hurok, S. *S. Hurok Presents: A Memoir of the Dance World*. New York: Hermitage House, 1953.

Isenberg, Barbara. *State of the Arts: California Artists Talk About Their Work*. Chicago, IL: Ivan R. Dee, 2000.

Juno, Andrea, editor. *Dangerous Drawings: Interviews with Comix and Graphix Artists*. New York: Juno Books, 1997.

Karkar, Jack and Waltraud, compilers and editors. *... And They Danced On*. Wausau, WI: Aardvark Enterprises, 1989.

Karsh, Yousuf. *Faces of Our Time*. Toronto and Buffalo, NY: University of Toronto Press, 1971.

Karsh, Yousuf. *Karsh: A Biography in Images*. Boston, MA: MFA Publications, 2003.

Kaufmann, Helen L. *Anecdotes of Music and Musicians*. New York: Grosset & Dunlap, Publishers, 1960.

Klosty, James, editor and photographer. *Merce Cunningham*. New York: Saturday Review Press/E.P. Dutton and Co., Inc, 1975.

Kristy, Davida. *George Balanchine: American Ballet Master*. Minneapolis, MN: Lerner Publications Company, 1996.

Krull, Kathleen. *Lives of the Artists: Masterpieces, Messes (and What the Neighbors Thought)*. San Diego, CA: Harcourt Brace & Company, 1995.

Ladré, Illaria Obidenna. *Illaria Obidenna Ladré: Memoirs of a Child of Theatre Street*. With Nancy Whyte. Seattle, WA: The Author, 1988.

Lahee, Henry C. *Famous Singers of To-day and Yesterday*. Boston: L.C. Page and Company, 1898.

Lavery, David, and Cynthia Burkhead, editors. *Joss Whedan Conversations*. Jackson, Mississippi: University Press of Mississippi, 2011.

Lawrence, Marjorie. *Interrupted Melody: The Story of My Life*. New York: Appleton-Century-Crofts, Inc., 1949.

Legat, Nicolas. *Ballet Russe: Memoirs of Nicolas Legat*. Translated by Sir Paul Dukes. London: Methuen & Co., Ltd., 1939.

Lehmann, Lotte. *Midway in My Song: The Autobiography of Lotte Lehmann*. Freeport, NY: Books for Libraries Press, 1970.

Levant, Oscar. *A Smattering of Ignorance*. New York: Doubleday, Doran, and Co., 1940.

Loyrette, Henri. *Degas: The Man and His Art*. New York: Abrams, 1993.

Main, Mary. *Isabel Allende: Award-Winning Latin American Author*. Berkeley Heights, NJ: Enslow Publishers, Inc., 2005.

Makarova, Natalia. *A Dance Autobiography*. Edited by Gennady Smakov. New York: Alfred A Knopf, Inc., 1979.

Mapleson, Colonel J.H. *The Mapleson Memoirs: The Career of an Operatic Impresario, 1858-1888*. Edited by Harold Rosenthal. New York: Appleton-Century, 1966.

Markova, Alicia. *Giselle and Me*. New York: The Vanguard Press, Inc., 1960.

Markova, Alicia. *Markova Remembers*. Boston, MA: Little, Brown and Company, 1986.

Martins, Peter. *Far From Denmark*. With Robert Cornfield. Boston/Toronto: Little, Brown and Company, 1982.

Massine, Léonide. *My Life in Ballet*. Edited by Phyllis Hartnoll and Robert Rubens. London: Macmillan and Co., Ltd., 1968.

Matthews, Denis. *In Pursuit of Music*. London: Victor Gollancz, Ltd., 1966.

Matz, Mary Jane. *Opera Stars in the Sun: Intimate Glimpses of Metropolitan Personalities*. New York: Farrar, Straus, and Cudahy, 1955.

Maybarduk, Linda. *The Dancer Who Flew: A Memoir of Rudolf Nureyev*. Toronto, Ontario, Canada: Tundra Books, 1999.

McArthur, Edwin. *Flagstad: A Personal Memoir*. New York: Alfred A. Knopf, 1965.

Meek, Harold. *Horn and Conductor: Reminiscences of a Practitioner with a Few Words of Advice*. Rochester, NY: University of Rochester Press, 1997.

Meltzer, Milton. *Carl Sandburg: A Biography*. Brookfield, CT: Twenty-First Century Books, 1999.

Mirriam-Goldberg, Caryn. *Sandra Cisneros: Latina Writer and Activist*. Berkeley Heights, NJ: Enslow Publishers, Inc., 1998.

Montague, Sarah. *Pas de Deux: Great Partnerships in Dance*. New York: Universe Books, 1981.

Moore, Dudley. *Musical Bumps*. London: Robson Books, 1986.

Mour, Stanley I. *American Jazz Musicians*. Springfield, NJ: Enslow Publications, Inc., 1998.

Neale, Wendy. *Ballet Life Behind the Scenes*. New York: Crown Publishers, Inc., 1982.

Newman, Barbara and Leslie E. Spatt. *Swan Lake*. London: Dance Books, 1983.

Nureyev, Rudolph. *Nureyev: An Autobiography with Pictures*. New York: E.P. Dutton and Co., Inc., 1963.

O'Connell, Charles. *The Other Side of the Record*. New York: Alfred A. Knopf, 1949.

O'Connor, Barbara. *Barefoot Dancer: The Story of Isadora Duncan*. Minneapolis, MN: Carolrhoda Books, Inc., 1994.

Orgill, Roxane. *Shout, Sister, Shout!* New York: Margaret K. McElderry Books, 2001.

Patelson, Alice. *Portrait of a Dancer, Memories of Balanchine: An Autobiography*. New York: Vantage Press, 1995.

Procter-Gregg, Humphrey. *Beecham Remembered*. London: Gerald Duckworth & Company Limited, 1976.

Robinson, Simon. *A Year With Rudolf Nureyev*. With Derek Robinson. London: Robert Hale Limited, 1997.

Rodriguez-Hunter, Suzanne. *Found Meals of the Lost Generation*. Boston, MA: Faber and Faber, 1994.

Rubin, Susan Goldman. *Wham! The Life and Times of Roy Lichtenstein*. New York: Abrams Books for Young Readers, 2008.

Russell, Anna. *I'm Not Making This Up, You Know: The Autobiography of the Queen of Musical Parody*. New York: The Continuum Publishing Company, 1985.

Rutkowska, Wanda. *Famous People in Anecdotes*. Warszawa: Wydawnictwa Szkolne i Pedagogiczne, 1977.

Savage, Richard Temple. *A Voice from the Pit*. Newton Abbot; North Pomfret, VT: David & Charles, 1988.

Shawn, Ted. *One Thousand and One Night Stands*. With Gray Poole. New York: Da Capo Press, Inc., 1979.

Sheridan, Martin. *Comics and Their Creators: Life Stories of American Cartoonists*. Westport, CT: Hyperion Press, Inc., 1977.

Shull, Jodie A. *Langston Hughes: "Life Makes Poems."* Berkeley Heights, New Jersey: Enslow Publishers, Inc., 2006.

Shull, Jodie A. *Pablo Neruda: Passion, Poetry, Politics*. Berkeley Heights, NJ: Enslow Publishers, Inc., 2009.

Slonimsky, Nicolas. *Slonimsky's Book of Musical Anecdotes*. New York and London: Routledge, 2002.

Swisher, Clarice. *Pablo Picasso*. San Diego, CA: Lucent Books, 1995.

Tallchief, Maria. *Maria Tallchief: America's Prima Ballerina*. With Larry Kaplan. New York: Henry Holt and Company, 1997.

Terry, Walter. *Star Performance: The Story of the World's Great Ballerinas*. Garden City, NY: Doubleday & Co., Inc., 1954.

Terry, Walter. *Ted Shawn: Father of American Dance*. New York: The Dial Press, 1976.

Tiel, Vicky. *It's All About the Dress*. New York: St. Martin's Press, 2011.

Vale, V., editor. *Zines! Volume 1*. San Francisco, CA: V/Search, 1996.

Voss, Frederick S. *Women of Our Time: An Album of Twentieth-Century Portraits*. London: Merrell in association with the National Portrait Gallery, Smithsonian Institution, 2002.

Waldron, Ann. *Claude Monet*. New York: Harry N. Abrams, Inc., 1991.

Weller, Sam. *Listen to the Echoes: The Ray Bradbury Interviews*. Brooklyn, NY: Melville House, 2010.

Wheatcroft, Andrew, compiler. *Dolin: Friends and Memories*. London and Henley: Routledge & Kegan Paul, 1982.

Whistler, James Abbott McNeill. *The Gentle Art of Making Enemies*. New York: Dover Publications, Inc., 1967.

Zoritch, George. *Ballet Mystique: Behind the Glamour of the Ballet Russe*. Mountain View, CA: Cynara Editions, 2000.

Appendix B: About the Author

It was a dark and stormy night. Suddenly a cry rang out, and on a hot summer night in 1954, Josephine, wife of Carl Bruce, gave birth to a boy — me. Unfortunately, this young married couple allowed Reuben Saturday, Josephine's brother, to name their first-born. Reuben, aka "The Joker," decided that Bruce was a nice name, so he decided to name me Bruce Bruce. I have gone by my middle name — David — ever since.

Being named Bruce David Bruce hasn't been all bad. Bank tellers remember me very quickly, so I don't often have to show an ID. It can be fun in charades, also. When I was a counselor as a teenager at Camp Echoing Hills in Warsaw, Ohio, a fellow counselor gave the signs for "sounds like" and "two words," then she pointed to a bruise on her leg twice. Bruise Bruise? Oh yeah, Bruce Bruce is the answer!

Uncle Reuben, by the way, gave me a haircut when I was in kindergarten. He cut my hair short and shaved a small bald spot on the back of my head. My mother wouldn't let me go to school until the bald spot grew out again.

Of all my brothers and sisters (six in all), I am the only transplant to Athens, Ohio. I was born in Newark, Ohio, and have lived all around Southeastern Ohio. However, I moved to Athens to go to Ohio University and have never left.

At Ohio U, I never could make up my mind whether to major in English or Philosophy, so I got a bachelor's degree with a double major in both areas, then I added a Master of Arts degree in English and a Master of Arts degree in Philosophy. Yes, I have my MAMA degree.

Currently, and for a long time to come (I eat fruits and veggies), I am spending my retirement writing books such as *Nadia Comaneci: Perfect 10*, *The Funniest People in Comedy*, *Homer's* Iliad: *A Retelling in Prose*, and *William Shakespeare's* Hamlet: *A Retelling in Prose*.

By the way, my sister Brenda Kennedy writes romances such as *A New Beginning* and *Shattered Dreams*.

Appendix C: Some Books by David Bruce

Anecdote Collections

250 Anecdotes About Opera
250 Anecdotes About Religion
250 Anecdotes About Religion: Volume 2
250 Music Anecdotes
Be a Work of Art: 250 Anecdotes and Stories
The Coolest People in Art: 250 Anecdotes
The Coolest People in the Arts: 250 Anecdotes
The Coolest People in Books: 250 Anecdotes
The Coolest People in Comedy: 250 Anecdotes
Create, Then Take a Break: 250 Anecdotes
Don't Fear the Reaper: 250 Anecdotes
The Funniest People in Art: 250 Anecdotes
The Funniest People in Books: 250 Anecdotes
The Funniest People in Books, Volume 2: 250 Anecdotes
The Funniest People in Books, Volume 3: 250 Anecdotes
The Funniest People in Comedy: 250 Anecdotes
The Funniest People in Dance: 250 Anecdotes
The Funniest People in Families: 250 Anecdotes
The Funniest People in Families, Volume 2: 250 Anecdotes
The Funniest People in Families, Volume 3: 250 Anecdotes
The Funniest People in Families, Volume 4: 250 Anecdotes
The Funniest People in Families, Volume 5: 250 Anecdotes
The Funniest People in Families, Volume 6: 250 Anecdotes
The Funniest People in Movies: 250 Anecdotes
The Funniest People in Music: 250 Anecdotes
The Funniest People in Music, Volume 2: 250 Anecdotes
The Funniest People in Music, Volume 3: 250 Anecdotes
The Funniest People in Neighborhoods: 250 Anecdotes
The Funniest People in Relationships: 250 Anecdotes
The Funniest People in Sports: 250 Anecdotes
The Funniest People in Sports, Volume 2: 250 Anecdotes
The Funniest People in Television and Radio: 250 Anecdotes
The Funniest People in Theater: 250 Anecdotes

The Funniest People Who Live Life: 250 Anecdotes
The Funniest People Who Live Life, Volume 2: 250 Anecdotes
The Kindest People Who Do Good Deeds, Volume 1: 250 Anecdotes
The Kindest People Who Do Good Deeds, Volume 2: 250 Anecdotes
Maximum Cool: 250 Anecdotes
The Most Interesting People in Movies: 250 Anecdotes
The Most Interesting People in Politics and History: 250 Anecdotes
The Most Interesting People in Politics and History, Volume 2: 250 Anecdotes
The Most Interesting People in Politics and History, Volume 3: 250 Anecdotes
The Most Interesting People in Religion: 250 Anecdotes
The Most Interesting People in Sports: 250 Anecdotes
The Most Interesting People Who Live Life: 250 Anecdotes
The Most Interesting People Who Live Life, Volume 2: 250 Anecdotes
Reality is Fabulous: 250 Anecdotes and Stories
Resist Psychic Death: 250 Anecdotes
Seize the Day: 250 Anecdotes and Stories

[1] Source: V. Vale, editor. *Zines! Volume 1*, pp. 77-82.

[2] Source: Yousuf Karsh, *Karsh: A Biography in Images*, p. 95.

[3] Source: Jan Greenberg and Sandra Jordan, *The American Eye: Eleven Artists of the Twentieth Century*, pp. 90-91.

[4] Source: James Barter, *Artists of the Renaissance*, p. 83.

[5] Source: Ann Waldron, *Claude Monet*, p. 46.

[6] Source: John Drew, *My Years on the Stage*, p. 200.

[7] Source: Walter Terry, *Ted Shawn: Father of American Dance*, p. 75.

[8] Source: David L. Groover and Cecil C. Conner, Jr., *Skeletons from the Opera Closet*, p. 152.

[9] Source: Denis Matthews, *In Pursuit of Music*, p. 119.

[10] Source: John Boyden, collector, *Stick to the Music: Scores of Orchestral Tales*, pp. 107-108.

[11] Source: George Zoritch, *Ballet Mystique: Behind the Glamour of the Ballet Russe*, p. 39.

[12] Source: Mary Main, *Isabel Allende: Award-Winning Latin American Author*, pp. 9-10, 17, 20, 37-38, 49, 71.

[13] Source: Virginia Brackett, Virginia. *A Home in the Heart: The Story of Sandra Cisneros*, pp. 14, 24-25.

[14] Source: Alicia Markova, *Giselle and Me*, p. 174.

[15] Source: Victor Borge and Robert Sherman, *My Favorite Comedies in Music*, p. 132.

[16] Source: Alexandra Danilova, *Choura*, p. 73.

[17] Source: Holly Brubach, *Ten Dancers*, p. 36.

[18] Source: David Ewen, *Famous Modern Conductors*, pp. 37, 82-83, 122.

[19] Source: Natalia Makarova, *A Dance Autobiography*, p. 18.

[20] Source: Susan Goldman Rubin, *Wham! The Life and Times of Roy Lichtenstein*, p. 3.

[21] Source: Illaria Obidenna Ladré, *Illaria Obidenna Ladré: Memoirs of a Child of Theatre Street*, p. 44.

[22] Source: Lotte Lehmann, *Midway in My Song*, pp. 12, 220.

[23] Source: Joseph Gale, *Behind Barres*, p. 54.

[24]Source: Mary Jane Matz, *Opera Stars in the Sun: Intimate Glimpses of Metropolitan Personalities*, p. 321.

[25]Source: Ted Shawn, *One Thousand and One Night Stands*, p. 53.

[26]Source: Anna Russell, *I'm Not Making This Up, You Know*, p. 161.

[27]Source: Nancy Van Norman Baer, *Bronislava Nijinska: A Dancer's Legacy*, pp. 16, 18.

[28]Source: Roxane Orgill, *Shout, Sister, Shout!*, pp. 59, 95.

[29]Source: Linda Maybarduk, *The Dancer Who Flew*, pp. 33, 141.

[30]Source: Robert Greskovic, *Ballet 101*, pp. xi, 191-192.

[31]Source: Natalia Makarova, *A Dance Autobiography*, p. 24.

[32]Source: Rudolph Nureyev, *Nureyev: An Autobiography with Pictures*, pp. 23, 65.

[33]Source: Alicia Markova, *Markova Remembers*, p. 169.

[34] Source: Vicky Tiel, *It's All About the Dress*, pp. 315-316.

[35]Source: Barbara Newman and Leslie E. Spatt, *Swan Lake*, p. 15.

[36]Source: Illaria Obidenna Ladré, *Illaria Obidenna Ladré: Memoirs of a Child of Theatre Street*, p. 7.

[37]Source: Alfred Werner, "Introduction" to James Abbott McNeill Whistler's *The Gentle Art of Making Enemies*, p. x.

[38]Source: Editors of *Dance Magazine*, with text by Gloria Manor, *The Gospel According to Dance*, p. 16.

[39] Source: V. Vale, editor. *Zines! Volume 1*, pp. 90-91.

[40] Source: Yousuf Karsh, *Karsh: A Biography in Images*, p. 93.

[41]Source: Suzanne Rodriguez-Hunter, *Found Meals of the Lost Generation*, pp. 14-15.

[42]Source: Colonel J. H. Mapleson, *The Mapleson Memoirs*, pp. 188-189.

[43]Source: Neville Cardus, editor, *Kathleen Ferrier: A Memoir*, pp. 14, 16-17, 49.

[44]Source: David W. Barber, *Bach, Beethoven, and the Boys*, pp. 53, 82, 84-85.

[45]Source: David W. Barber, *Bach, Beethoven, and the Boys*, pp. 143, 145.

[46] Source: Victor Borge and Robert Sherman, *My Favorite Intermissions*, p. 24.

[47]Source: Frances Alda, *Men, Women, and Tenors*, pp. 86, 88.

[48]Source: John Boyden, collector, *Stick to the Music: Scores of Orchestral Tales*, pp. 35-36.

[49]Source: Harold Meek, *Horn and Conductor*, p. 23.

[50]Source: Thomas Beecham, *A Mingled Chime*, p. 190.

[51]Source: Laning Humphrey, compiler, *The Humor of Music and Other Oddities in the Art*, pp. 25, 92.

[52]Source: Samuel Chotzinoff, *Toscanini: An Intimate Portrait*, p. 23.

[53]Source: David Ewen, *Dictators of the Baton*, pp. 53, 55-56.

[54]Source: Helen L. Kaufmann, *Anecdotes of Music and Musicians*, p. 268.

[55] Source: *Anton Seidl: A Memorial by His Friends*, p. 164.

[56]Source: Dudley Moore, *Musical Bumps*, p. 81.

[57] Source: Barbara Isenberg, *State of the Arts: California Artists Talk About Their Work*, pp. 96-97.

[58]Source: Simon Doonan, *Confessions of a Window Dresser*, p. 197.

[59] Source: Guerrilla Girls, *Confessions of the Guerilla Girls*, pp. 15, 19, 22.

[60] Source: Milton Meltzer, *Carl Sandburg: A Biography*, pp. 54, 56.

[61] Source: Germaine Greer, "Now please pay attention, everybody. I'm about to tell you what art is." *The Guardian*. 6 March 2011 <http://www.guardian.co.uk/artanddesign/2011/mar/06/germaine-greer-art-graffiti>.

[62]Source: Barbara O'Connor, *Barefoot Dancer: The Story of Isadora Duncan*, pp. 7, 14.

[63] Source: Nicolas Slonimsky, *Slonimsky's Book of Musical Anecdotes*, pp. 44-45.

[64]Source: Ted Cott, *The Victor Book of Musical Fun*, pp. 50, 104.

[65]Source: Henry T. Finck, *Musical Laughs*, p. 88.

[66]Source: Andrew Wheatcroft, compiler, *Dolin: Friends and Memories*, pages are unnumbered.

[67] Source: Yousuf Karsh, *Faces of Our Time*, pp. 185-187.

[68]Source: Frances Alda, *Men, Women, and Tenors*, pp. 11-12.

[69]Source: Wanda Rutkowska, *Famous People in Anecdotes*, pp. 66-67.

[70]Source: Herbert Furst, *The New Anecdotes of Painters and Paintings*, p. 37.

[71]Source: Francis A. Davis, *Frank Lloyd Wright: Maverick Architect*, p. 73.

[72]Source: Cyril W. Beaumont, *Vaslav Nijinsky*, pp. 19-21, 28.

[73]Source: Editors of *Dance Magazine*, with text by Gloria Manor, *The Gospel According to Dance*, pp. 40, 42, 91, 94, 106.

[74]Source: Cynthia Gregory, *Cynthia Gregory Dances Swan Lake*, pp. 11, 30, 39.

[75]Source: Suzanne Farrell, *Holding On to the Air*, p. 263.

[76]Source: Frank Augustyn and Shelley Tanaka, *Footnotes: Dancing the World's Best-Loved Ballets*, pp. 37-38, 67.

[77]Source: Sarah Montague, *Pas de Deux*, p. 99.

[78]Source: Alice Patelson, *Portrait of a Dancer, Memories of Balanchine*, pp. 46-47.

[79]Source: Alexandra Danilova, *Choura*, p. 173.

[80]Source: John Gregory, editor, *Heritage of a Ballet Master*, pp. 25, 29, 31.

[81]Source: John Gruen, *People Who Dance*, p. 47.

[82]Source: Davida Kristy, *George Balanchine: American Ballet Master*, p. 108.

[83]Source: David Goodnough, *Pablo Casals: Cellist for the World*, pp. 72, 74, 116.

[84] Source: David Lavery, and Cynthia Burkhead, editors, *Joss Whedan Conversations*, pp. 62-63, 140.

[85]Source: Mary Garden and Louis Biancolli, *Mary Garden's Story*, p. 12.

[86] Source: Jodie A. Shull, *Langston Hughes: "Life Makes Poems,"* pp. 15, 18, 20, 42.

[87] Source: Susan Goldman Rubin, *Wham! The Life and Times of Roy Lichtenstein*, pp. 12-13, 15.

[88]Source: Peter Martins, *Far From Denmark*, pp. 159, 168, 194.

[89] Source: Barbara Isenberg, *State of the Arts: California Artists Talk About Their Work*, pp. 66-67.

[90]Source: Jack and Waltraud Karkar, compilers and editors, ... *And They Danced On*, p. 50.

[91]Source: John Gregory, editor, *Heritage of a Ballet Master*, pp. 18, 29.

[92]Source: John Gruen, *People Who Dance*, p. 153.

[93]Source: Mary Garden and Louis Biancolli, *Mary Garden's Story*, pp. 16-17.

[94]Source: Rose Heylbut and Aime Gerber, *Backstage at the Opera*, pp. 131, 134.

[95]Source: Wendie C. Old, *Duke Ellington: Giant of Jazz*, p. 18.

[96]Source: Nicolas Legat, *Ballet Russe*, p. 16.

[97]Source: Jan Greenberg and Sandra Jordan, *Vincent van Gogh: Portrait of an Artist*, pp. 42-43.

[98]Source: S. Hurok, *S. Hurok Presents*, p. 96.

[99] Source: John Drew, *My Years on the Stage*, pp. 86-87.

[100]Source: Clarice Swisher, *Pablo Picasso*, pp. 88-89.

[101] Source: Sam Weller, *Listen to the Echoes: The Ray Bradbury Interviews*, pp. 77-80, 125-126.

[102] Source: Andrea Juno, editor. *Dangerous Drawings: Interviews with Comix and Graphix Artists*, p. 154.

[103]Source: Alicia Markova, *Giselle and Me*, p. 109.

[104] Source: Caryn Mirriam-Goldberg, *Sandra Cisneros: Latina Writer and Activist*, pp. 5, 7, 28, 32, 37-38, 82.

[105]Source: Anton Dolin, *Alicia Markova: Her Life and Art*, pp. 43-46.

[106]Source: Spring Hermann, *R.C. Gorman: Navaho Artist*, pp. 28-29, 44.

[107] Source: William J. Boerst, *Isaac Asimov: Writer of the Future*, pp. 16, 20.

[108]Source: Margot Fonteyn, *Autobiography*, p. 201.

[109]Source: Margot Fonteyn, presenter, *Pavlova: Portrait of a Dancer*, p. 68.

[110] Source: Simon Doonan, *Eccentric Glamour*, pp. 207-208.

[111]Source: Sarah Giles, *Fred Astaire: His Friends Talk*, pp. 14, 52, 56.

[112]Source: James Klosty, editor and photographer, *Merce Cunningham*, p. 58.

[113]Source: Sarah Giles, *Fred Astaire: His Friends Talk*, p. 156.

[114] Source: Oscar Rickett, "This much I know: Edmund White." *Guardian* (UK). 14 January 2012 <http://www.guardian.co.uk/lifeandstyle/2012/jan/15/this-much-know-edmund-white>.

[115]Source: Simon Robinson, *A Year With Rudolf Nureyev*, p. 166.

[116] Source: Gerald Scarfe, "Ronald Searle: Now let's have some fizz." *Guardian* (UK). 3 January 2012 <http://www.guardian.co.uk/artanddesign/2012/jan/03/ronald-searle-gerald-scarfe>.

[117]Source: Marjorie Lawrence, *Interrupted Melody: The Story of My Life*, p. 158.

[118] Source: *Anton Seidl: A Memorial by His Friends*, pp. 19, 41, 54, 58.

[119]Source: David Ewen, *Dictators of the Baton*, pp. 119-120.

[120] Source: William J. Boerst, *Generous Anger: The Story of George Orwell*, pp. 78, 87-88.

[121]Source: Dorothy Caruso, *Enrico Caruso: His Life and Death*, pp. 87, 146.

[122]Source: Agnes de Mille, *Portrait Gallery*, p. 9.

[123]Source: Sir Rudolf Bing, *5000 Nights at the Opera*, p. 26.

[124]Source: Colonel J. H. Mapleson, *The Mapleson Memoirs*, p. 162.

[125]Source: Henry C. Lahee, *Famous Singers of To-day and Yesterday*, pp. 166-167.

[126]Source: Simon Doonan, *Confessions of a Window Dresser*, pp. 160-161.

[127]Source: Margot Fonteyn, *Autobiography*, p. 257.

[128]Source: Doreen Gonzales, *Diego Rivera: His Art, His Life*, p. 105.

[129]Source: Margaret F. Atkinson and May Hillman, *Dancers of the Ballet*, p. 160.

[130]Source: Henry C. Lahee, *Famous Singers of To-day and Yesterday*, pp. 21-22.

[131]Source: Oscar Levant, *A Smattering of Ignorance*, p. ix.

[132]Source: Léonide Massine, *My Life in Ballet*, p. 254.

[133]Source: Lotte Lehmann, *Midway in My Song*, p. 105.

[134]Source: Barry Hewlett-Davies, *A Night at the Opera*, p. 29.

[135]Source: Leslie Ayre, *The Wit of Music*, pp. 24, 42, 54, 77.

[136]Source: Rusty E. Frank, *Tap!*, p. 70.

[137]Source: Nicolas Legat, *Ballet Russe*, p. 22.

[138]Source: Laning Humphrey, compiler, *The Humor of Music and Other Oddities in the Art*, p. 13.

[139]Source: Samuel Chotzinoff, *Toscanini: An Intimate Portrait*, pp. 4-6.

[140]Source: Jim Haskins and N.R. Mitgang, *Mr. Bojangles*, pp. 209-210.

[141] Source: Frederick S. Voss, *Women of Our Time: An Album of Twentieth-Century Portraits*, pp. 112-113.

[142]Source: Ted Shawn, *One Thousand and One Night Stands*, p. 95.

[143] Source: William J. Boerst, *Isaac Asimov: Writer of the Future*, pp. 44, 75.

[144]Source: Marjorie Lawrence, *Interrupted Melody: The Story of My Life*, pp. 6-7.

[145]Source: Wendy Neale, *Ballet Life Behind the Scenes*, p. 111.

[146]Source: Linda Maybarduk, *The Dancer Who Flew*, pp. 105-106, 144.

[147]Source: Jack and Waltraud Karkar, compilers and editors, ... *And They Danced On*, p. 196.

[148]Source: A.H. Franks, editor, *Pavlova: A Collection of Memoirs*, pp. 14, 70-71.

[149]Source: Sarah Montague, *Pas de Deux*, p. 37.

[150]Source: Alicia Markova, *Markova Remembers*, p. 128.

[151]Source: Walter Terry, *Star Performance*, p. 128.

[152] Source: Henry T. Finck, *My Adventures in the Golden Age of Music*, p. 180.

[153]Source: A.H. Franks, editor, *Pavlova: A Collection of Memoirs*, pp. 38-39.

[154]Source: Richard Temple Savage, *A Voice from the Pit*, p. 83.

[155]Source: Nigel Douglas, *More Legendary Voices*, p. 215.

[156] Source: Martin Sheridan, *Comics and Their Creators: Life Stories of American Cartoonists*, pp. 60-61.

[157]Source: Robert Greskovic, *Ballet 101*, p. 167.

[158]Source: Mary Jane Matz, *Opera Stars in the Sun: Intimate Glimpses of Metropolitan Personalities*, pp. 336-337.

[159]Source: Frank Augustyn and Shelley Tanaka, *Footnotes: Dancing the World's Best-Loved Ballets*, p. 59.

[160]Source: Neville Cardus, editor, *Kathleen Ferrier: A Memoir*, p. 50.

[161] Source: *Anecdotes of the Hour By Famous Men*, p. 17.

[162] Source: Henry T. Finck, *My Adventures in the Golden Age of Music*, p. 211.

[163] Source: *Anecdotes of the Hour By Famous Men*, p. 15.

[164]Source: Edwin McArthur, *Flagstad: A Personal Memoir*, pp. 5, 199.

[165]Source: Henry T. Finck, *Musical Laughs*, pp. 114-115.

[166] Source: Henri Loyrette, *Degas: The Man and His Art*, p. 169.

[167]Source: Spring Hermann, *R.C. Gorman: Navaho Artist*, pp. 46-47.

[168]Source: Wanda Rutkowska, *Famous People in Anecdotes*, pp. 38-39.

[169] Source: Sam Weller, *Listen to the Echoes: The Ray Bradbury Interviews*, pp. 208-209.

[170]Source: Leslie Ayre, *The Wit of Music*, pp. 45-46.

[171]Source: Jan Greenberg and Sandra Jordan, *Vincent van Gogh: Portrait of an Artist*, p. 57.

[172] Source: Maria Tallchief, *Maria Tallchief: America's Prima Ballerina*, pp. 87-98.

[173]Source: James Klosty, editor and photographer, *Merce Cunningham*, p. 66.

[174]Source: Clarice Swisher, *Pablo Picasso*, p. 75.

[175]Source: David W. Barber, *Getting a Handel on Messiah*, p. 38.

[176]Source: Andrew Wheatcroft, compiler, *Dolin: Friends and Memories*, pages are unnumbered.

[177]Source: Kathleen Krull, *Lives of the Artists*, p. 71.

[178] Source: Yousuf Karsh, *Faces of Our Time*, pp. 165-167.

[179]Source: Ann Waldron, *Claude Monet*, p. 60.

[180] Source: Roger Ebert, "Beat the Devil." *Chicago Sun-Times*. 26 November 2000 <http://rogerebert.suntimes.com/apps/pbcs.dll/ article?AID=%2F20001126%2FREVIEWS08%2F11260301%2F1023&AID1=&AID2= Also: Roger Ebert, "John Huston: 'It's as bad to be ahead of your time as behind it.'" *Chicago Sun-Times*. 27 August 1975 <http://rogerebert.suntimes.com/apps/ pbcs.dll/article?AID=/19750827/PEOPLE/508270301/1023>.

[181]Source: Léonide Massine, *My Life in Ballet*, pp. 233-234.

[182]Source: Rusty E. Frank, *Tap!*, p. 82.

[183]Source: Agnes de Mille, *Portrait Gallery*, p. 110.

[184]Source: Harold Meek, *Horn and Conductor*, p. 79.

[185] Source: William J. Boerst, *Generous Anger: The Story of George Orwell*, pp. 34, 36, 84.

[186] Source: Maria Tallchief, *Maria Tallchief: America's Prima Ballerina*, pp. 14-15, 27, 236-237.

[187]Source: David W. Barber, *Getting a Handel on Messiah*, pp. 43-44.

[188]Source: Carin T. Ford, *Legends of American Dance and Choreography*, pp. 4, 35, 39-40.

[189]Source: Francis A. Davis, *Frank Lloyd Wright: Maverick Architect*, pp. 11, 23.

[190]Source: Rose Heylbut and Aimé Gerber, *Backstage at the Opera*, pp. 173-174.

[191]Source: Barry Hewlett-Davies, *A Night at the Opera*, p. 113.

[192]Source: Helen L. Kaufmann, *Anecdotes of Music and Musicians*, p. 20.

[193] Source: Jodie A. Shull, *Pablo Neruda: Passion, Poetry, Politics*, pp. 19, 78, 87-88, 97, 105.

[194] Source: Jodie A. Shull, *Langston Hughes: "Life Makes Poems,"* pp. 4-7.

[195]Source: Wendie C. Old, *Louis Armstrong: King of Jazz*, pp. 20, 24-25, 58, 79, 115.

[196]Source: Jim Haskins and N.R. Mitgang, *Mr. Bojangles*, pp. 160, 164, 233.

[197]Source: Stanley I. Mour, *American Jazz Musicians*, pp. 51-52.

[198]Source: Oscar Levant, *A Smattering of Ignorance*, pp. 22-23, 262.

[199] Source: Roger Ebert, "Smash his camera, but not immediately." Blogs.suntimes.com. 25 January 2010 <http://blogs.suntimes.com/ebert/2010/01/ smash_his_camera_but_not_immed.html>.

[200]Source: Thomas Beecham, *A Mingled Chime*, pp. 106-107.

[201]Source: Anton Dolin, *Alicia Markova: Her Life and Art*, pp. 85-88.

[202]Source: Davida Kristy, *George Balanchine: American Ballet Master*, pp. 81, 95.

[203]Source: Wendy Neale, *Ballet Life Behind the Scenes*, p. 33.

[204]Source: Dorothy Caruso, *Enrico Caruso: His Life and Death*, pp. 70, 157.

[205]Source: Simon Robinson, *A Year With Rudolf Nureyev*, pp. 51-52.

[206]Source: Charles O'Connell, *The Other Side of the Record*, p. 87.

[207]Source: Stanley I. Mour, *American Jazz Musicians*, pp. 60, 90.

[208] Source: Holly Brubach, *Ten Dancers*, p. 95.

[209]Source: David L. Groover and Cecil C. Conner, Jr., *Skeletons from the Opera Closet*, p. 126.

[210] Source: Victor Borge and Robert Sherman, *My Favorite Intermissions*, p. 25.

[211]Source: Plácido Domingo, *My First Forty Years*, p. 83.

[212]Source: Carin T. Ford, *Legends of American Dance and Choreography*, pp. 33-34.

[213]Source: S. Hurok, *S. Hurok Presents*, p. 113.

[214]Source: Richard Temple Savage, *A Voice from the Pit*, p. 48.

[215]Source: Sir Rudolf Bing, *5000 Nights at the Opera*, p. 87.

[216]Source: Kathleen Krull, *Lives of the Artists*, p. 56.

[217]Source: Walter Terry, *Ted Shawn: Father of American Dance*, p. 39.

[218]Source: Walter Terry, *Ted Shawn: Father of American Dance*, p. 5.

[219]Source: Suzanne Farrell, *Holding On to the Air*, pp. 38, 64.

[220]Source: Nigel Douglas, *More Legendary Voices*, p. 21.

[221]Source: Victor Borge and Robert Sherman, *My Favorite Comedies in Music*, p. 87.

[222] Source: Vicky Tiel, *It's All About the Dress*, pp. 296-298.

[223]Source: David Goodnough, *Pablo Casals: Cellist for the World*, pp. 59-60.

[224]Source: Charles O'Connell, *The Other Side of the Record*, p. 45.

[225]Source: Clive Barnes, *Inside American Ballet Theatre*, p. 83.

[226]Source: Denis Matthews, *In Pursuit of Music*, pp. 68, 81.

[227]Source: Evangelia Callas, *My Daughter Maria Callas*, pp. 18, 32.

[228]Source: Jan Greenberg and Sandra Jordan, *The American Eye: Eleven Artists of the Twentieth Century*, p. 73.

[229] Source: Simon Doonan, *Eccentric Glamour*, pp. 197-200.

[230]Source: Margaret F. Atkinson and May Hillman, *Dancers of the Ballet*, p. 45.

[231] Source: Guerrilla Girls, *Confessions of the Guerilla Girls*, p. 24.

[232]Source: Dudley Moore, *Musical Bumps*, pp. 46, 146.

[233]Source: George Zoritch, *Ballet Mystique: Behind the Glamour of the Ballet Russe*, pp. 26, 242, 256.

[234] Source: Nicolas Slonimsky, *Slonimsky's Book of Musical Anecdotes*, pp. 17, 29.

[235]Source: Cath Carroll, *Tom Waits*, pp. 51, 58.

[236]Source: Humphrey Procter-Gregg, *Beecham Remembered*, p. 40.

[237]Source: Ted Cott, *The Victor Book of Musical Fun*, p. 87.

[238] Source: Christina Binkley, "The Serious Business of Pretty Pink Things." *Wall Street Journal.* 18 June 2011 <http://online.wsj.com/article/ SB10001424052702304186404576386743960163676.html?mod=WSJ_LifeStyle_LifeSty

[239] Source: Milton Meltzer, *Carl Sandburg: A Biography*, pp. 15, 18, 20, 27, 33.

[240] Source: Andrea Juno, editor. *Dangerous Drawings: Interviews with Comix and Graphix Artists*, pp. 207-208.

[241] Source: Anna Russell, *I'm Not Making This Up, You Know*, p. 239.

[242] Source: Plácido Domingo, *My First Forty Years*, p. 86.

[243] Source: Humphrey Procter-Gregg, *Beecham Remembered*, p. 61.

[244] Source: Wendie C. Old, *Duke Ellington: Giant of Jazz*, pp. 46-47.

[245] Source: Henri Loyrette, *Degas: The Man and His Art*, p. 157.

[246] Source: Doreen Gonzales, *Diego Rivera: His Art, His Life*, pp. 61, 75.

[247] Source: Alice Patelson, *Portrait of a Dancer, Memories of Balanchine*, p. 48.

[248] Source: Martin Sheridan, *Comics and Their Creators: Life Stories of American Cartoonists*, p. 178.

[249] Source: Barbara Newman and Leslie E. Spatt, *Swan Lake*, pp. 59-60.

[250] Source: William Cubberley and Joseph Carmen, *Round About the Ballet*, p. 208.

www.ingramcontent.com/pod-product-compliance
Lightning Source LLC
Chambersburg PA
CBHW051237160726
47994CB00002B/923

9798215993583